EMERIL LAGASSE FRENCH DOOR 360 DUAL ZONE AIR FRYER COOKBOOK

1500 Days of Easy-to-Follow, Budget-Friendly & Delicious Fryer Recipes to Enjoy With Your Family and Friends incl. 30-Day Meal Plan

William Bernard

TABLE OF
CONTENT

INTRODUCTION

Are you tired of the kitchen shuffle, trying to find space for all your favorite ingredients in a cramped air fryer? I feel your pain. Picture this: you're excited to whip up a delicious, crispy, and healthier meal in your air fryer, but the limited space feels like it's cramping your culinary style. If this sounds all too familiar, I've got some fantastic news for you!

I used to be in the same predicament until I discovered a game-changer in the world of air frying: the Emeril Lagasse French Door 360 Dual Zone Air Fryer. Trust me when I say this air fryer is nothing short of a kitchen revolution. It's not just a tool; it's a culinary partner that unlocks endless possibili-ties.

Imagine having a treasure trove of mouthwatering recipes at your fingertips, specially crafted for the Emeril Lagasse French Door 360 Dual Zone Air Fryer. From appetizers that'll make your taste buds dance to main courses that redefine what's possible with air frying, and don't even get me started on the delectable desserts – this cookbook is your gateway to culinary mastery.

So, whether you're a seasoned home chef looking to up your game or a new-bie eager to explore the world of air frying, the Emeril Lagasse French Door 360 Dual Zone Air Fryer Cookbook is here to guide you every step of the way. Get ready to transform your kitchen into a flavor-packed adventure, one recipe at a time. Let's dive in!

CHAPTER 1

THE EMERIL LAGASSE FRENCH DOOR 360 AIR FRYER BASICS

Introducing the Emeril Lagasse Everyday French Door 360 Air Fryer, a culinary powerhouse with a 25-quart capacity and the unique ability to cook in two different ways simultaneously. Crafted with precision in stainless steel, this kitchen marvel not only elevates your cooking experience but also adds a touch of sophistication to your kitchen decor. With its dual-temperature zone feature, you can unlock a world of culinary possibilities, making meal preparation more versatile and efficient than ever before. Whether you're crisping up fries or roasting a succulent chicken, the Emeril Lagasse Everyday French Door 360 Air Fryer is your trusted companion for achieving delicious results effortlessly.

Using the Control Panel

When utilizing the Emeril Dual Zone air fryer, you'll interact with its control panel, which offers various functions to customize your cooking experience.

Selecting Cooking Presets
Begin by using the "Program Selection Knob" to pick a cooking preset from the options listed in the "Preset Chart" section. As you turn the knob, the corresponding preset on the control panel will light up.

Display Information
The control panel provides essential information about the cooking process. The "Fan Display" illuminates when the fan is running, while the "Heating Element Display" lights up when heating elements are active. The "Temperature Display" shows the current cooking temperature, and the "Time Display" indicates preheating or remaining cooking time. The "Mute Display" indicates the Mute Function status.

Temperature Adjustment
Override preset temperatures by pressing the "Temperature Button" and turning the dial to make temperature adjustments. Switch between Fahrenheit and Celsius by holding the Temperature Button.

Fan Control
Activate or deactivate the fan and adjust its speed by pressing the "Fan Button." Fan adjustments are typically possible after starting a cooking preset. For manual cool-down after a cooking cycle, hold the Fan Button for 3 seconds.

Time Adjustment
Adjust preset times by pressing the "Time Button" and turning the dial.

Interior Light
Illuminate the appliance's interior at any time during cooking by pressing the "Light Button."

Mute Function
Enable or disable the Mute Function by pressing and holding the "Light Button" for 3 seconds. When activated, it mutes beeping sounds associated with programming functions and the end-of-cooking cycle alert.

Starting and Pausing
Press the "Start/Pause Button" to initiate or pause the cooking process.

Cancellation
Stop the cooking process at any time by selecting the "Cancel Button." Holding it for 3 seconds powers off the appliance entirely.

Control Knob
Utilize the "Control Knob" to navigate and select preset modes. The knob's ring lights blue when the appliance is on, turns red when a preset is chosen, and returns to blue upon completing the cooking cycle.

Benefits of Emeril Lagasse French Door

The Emeril Air Fryer offers a multitude of benefits that elevate your everyday cooking experience:
1. Versatility at its Best: This XL 25-Qt. air fryer oven is a game-changer, combining the functionalities

of 10 kitchen appliances into one compact countertop cooker. It's incredibly versatile, making it an ideal addition to your kitchen arsenal.

2. Dual Cooking Zones: With dual temperature zones, you can cook two different foods in two distinct ways at the same time. Custom settings for each zone ensure that your main dish and sides are prepared exactly to your liking, providing ultimate culinary flexibility.

3. Streamlined Cooking: Thanks to QuickSync Technology, there's no need for back-to-back cooking. This innovative feature syncs cooking times and settings in each zone, ensuring that your entire meal is ready simultaneously, eliminating the hassle of juggling multiple cooking processes.

4. Speed and Efficiency: The Emeril Air Fryer is designed to save you time in the kitchen. It can prepare family-sized meals up to 60% faster than traditional cooking methods. The XL 25-Qt. capacity oven provides ample space, and you can even remove the divider for extra-large, full-zone cooking.

5. Frozen to Fabulous in Minutes: Say goodbye to time-consuming defrosting. With this air fryer, you can go from frozen to finished in just 10 minutes. Whether it's frozen shrimp or a delectable scampi, you can cook straight from the freezer, making meal preparation quicker and more convenient than ever before.

How to Use the Air Fryer?

Before using your appliance, ensure it's positioned on a stable, level, and heat-resistant surface. This not only provides a secure cooking environment but also prevents any wobbling or instability during operation. Furthermore, choose a location with good air circulation to maintain proper ventilation, which aids in the appliance's cooling process. Keep it away from hot surfaces, other objects, or appliances, as well as any materials that could potentially combust when exposed to heat.

Power Outlet:
To ensure the appliance functions correctly, make sure it's plugged into a dedicated power outlet. This dedicated connection helps maintain a consistent power supply, which is crucial for the appliance to perform efficiently and reliably.

Accessory Selection:

Selecting the appropriate cooking accessory is key to achieving your desired culinary results. Different recipes and cooking methods may require specific accessories, such as the Oven Rack, Baking Pan, or Crisper Tray. Choosing the right one for your dish ensures even cooking and optimal performance.

Loading Food:
Before you begin cooking, place the food you wish to prepare inside the appliance. Ensure that the doors are securely closed to maintain the cooking environment and allow for even heat distribution. A secure closure helps retain heat and ensures the cooking process proceeds as intended.

Selecting Preset Mode:
Using the Control Knob, you can scroll through the available presets to find the one that best suits your dish. Once you've made your selection, press the Start/Pause Button to initiate the cooking cycle. It's worth noting that some presets may include a preheating feature, which can be referred to in the "Preset Chart" section for more information.

Adjusting Settings:
The appliance provides flexibility during cooking. After the cooking cycle has started, you can make adjustments to achieve your desired outcome. Use the Temperature Button and Control Knob to modify the cooking temperature, or use the Time Button and Control Knob to change the cooking duration. These adjustments empower you to tailor your cooking experience to your specific needs.

When toasting bread or a bagel, you can control the lightness or darkness of the final product using the same knobs. Additionally, the appliance will signal the end of the cooking process with a series of beeps, notifying you that the cooking time has elapsed. If the appliance remains untouched for 3 minutes, it will automatically turn off, enhancing safety.

Safety is paramount. The appliance generates intense heat during cooking, making all surfaces, both inside and outside, extremely hot. To avoid injury, always wear oven mitts when handling hot components. Furthermore, it's essential to allow the appliance to cool for at least 30 minutes before attempting to clean or store it.

Using the Accessories

The Emeril Dual Zone Air Fryer offers a multitude of accessories that elevate its versatility in the kitchen. These accessories are designed to enhance your cooking experience in various ways.

Oven Rack:
To use the Oven Rack with your Emeril Air Fryer, start by inserting the Drip Tray below the bottom heating elements, located at the very bottom of the appliance. Then, refer to the markings on the appliance's door to choose the recommended cooking position for your specific recipe. Next, place your food onto the Oven Rack and insert the rack into the given slots.

Baking Pan:
Utilizing the Baking Pan involves similar steps. Begin by inserting the Drip Tray beneath the bottom heating elements. Select the shelf position recommended for your recipe using the markings on the appliance's door. Place your food onto the Baking Pan and insert it into the chosen slot. Like the Oven Rack, the Baking Pan can be positioned under the Crisper Tray or Oven Rack to capture dripping juices and reduce smoke, as outlined in the "Recommended Accessory Positions" section.

Crisper Tray:
The Crisper Tray is another accessory option. Insert the Drip Tray beneath the bottom heating elements, just as with the previous accessories. Then, choose the recommended shelf position for your recipe using the door markings. Place your food onto the Crisper Tray and insert it into the designated slot. To minimize drippings and smoke when cooking foods prone to dripping, such as bacon or steak, consider using the Baking Pan below the Crisper Tray or Oven Rack, following the guidance provided in the "Recommended Accessory Positions" section.

Grill Plate Handle:
When using the Grill Plate, insert the Drip Tray beneath the bottom heating elements. Position your food on the Grill Plate and insert it into the recommended shelf position. To remove the accessory, employ the Grill Plate Handle. First, use the larger connected hook to hook the top part of the accessory, pulling it slightly out of the appliance. Then, flip the Grill Plate Handle over and utilize the two smaller hooks to latch it to the accessory. Pull the accessory out and place it on a heat-resistant surface. Remember to avoid touching hot accessories with your bare hands and exercise caution during handling. Additionally, refrain from using the Grill Plate Handle to carry the Crisper Tray or Grill Plate.

Rotisserie Spit:
To utilize the Rotisserie Spit, start by placing the Drip Tray underneath the lower heating elements. Next, take out the Forks and proceed to thread the Rotisserie Spit lengthwise through the center of your food item. Attach the Forks on both sides of the Spit and firmly secure them using the Set Screws. For enhanced stability, ensure that the Rotisserie Forks are inserted into the food at varying angles. To install the Rotisserie Spit within the appliance, hold it at a slight tilt, with the left side positioned higher than the right. Insert the right side of the Spit into the Rotisserie connection located inside the appliance and then secure the left side into the corresponding Rotisserie connection on the appliance's left side.

Removing the Rotisserie Spit Section:
With the Fetch Tool in hand, engage the lower sections of the shaft linked to the Rotisserie Spit on both the left and right sides. Gradually exert a gentle force to the left to disengage the Rotisserie Spit from the Rotisserie Socket. Proceed with caution as you extract the Rotisserie Spit from the appliance. When it comes to separating the food from the Rotisserie Spit, twist and loosen the screws on one of the Rotisserie Forks, and then repeat the process to detach the second Rotisserie Fork. Glide the food off the Rotisserie Spit.

These instructions guide you through the proper use of various accessories for your Emeril Air Fryer, ensuring both effectiveness and safety in your cooking endeavors.

How to Clean the Air Fryer

To maintain the performance and hygiene of your Emeril Air Fryer, it's crucial to clean it after each use. Here's a step-by-step guide on how to clean it effectively:

1. Safety Precautions:
Before starting the cleaning process, ensure the appliance is completely cooled down. Unplug it from the wall socket to prevent any electrical hazards during cleaning.

2. Exterior Cleaning:
Begin by wiping the outside of the appliance using a warm, moist cloth and a mild detergent. This step helps remove any grease or residue that might have accumulated during cooking.

3. Cleaning the Doors:
Gently scrub both sides of the appliance doors with warm, soapy water and a damp cloth. Ensure a thorough cleaning of both the interior and exterior of the doors. Avoid soaking or submerging the appliance in water, and refrain from using a dishwasher for this task.

4. Interior Cleaning:
Clean the inside of the appliance with hot water, a mild detergent, and a nonabrasive sponge. Be cautious not to scrub the delicate heating coils, as they can break if mishandled. After cleaning, rinse the appliance thoroughly with a clean, damp cloth to eliminate any soap residue. Ensure there is no standing water inside the appliance.

5. Removing Food Residue:
For any stubborn or unwanted food residue inside the appliance, utilize a nonabrasive cleaning brush to gently eliminate it.

6. Accessories Cleaning:
In the case of caked-on food residue on accessories such as trays or plates, soak them in warm, soapy water to loosen the food particles. It's recommended to hand-wash these accessories for a thorough cleaning.

7. Final Steps:
Unplug the appliance once more and allow it to cool down entirely. Confirm that all components, including trays, plates, and accessories, are clean and completely dry before storing them. Store the appliance in a clean, dry place to prevent the accumulation of dust or debris.

FAQs about the Emeril Lagasse French Door

1. Is Preheating Required?
Certainly! The appliance features an intelligent preheating function that ensures it reaches the preset cooking temperature before the countdown timer begins. This convenient feature is active for all preprogrammed settings, except for Toast, Slow Cook, and Dehydrate.

2. Can I Pause the Cooking Cycle?
Absolutely! You have control over the cooking process. Simply press the Cancel Button, and the cooking cycle will come to a halt, allowing you to adjust as needed.

3. Can I Turn Off the Appliance Mid-Cycle?
Yes, you have the flexibility to shut off the appliance at any moment. Just hold down the Cancel Button for 3 seconds, and the appliance will power down promptly.

4. Can I Monitor the Cooking Progress?
Certainly! Keeping an eye on your cooking is easy. You can check the progress by pressing the Light Button to illuminate the interior or by pressing the Start/Pause Button and then opening the door for a quick look.

CHAPTER 2
BREAKFAST

Ham and Corn Muffins

PREP TIME: 10 minutes
COOK TIME: 10 minutes

2 tbsps. canola oil
¾ cup yellow cornmeal
1 egg, beaten
½ cup milk
½ cup shredded sharp Cheddar cheese
½ cup diced ham
¼ cup flour
1½ tsps. baking powder
¼ tsp. salt

1. In a medium bowl, stir together the flour, cornmeal, baking powder and salt.
2. Add the egg, canola oil, and milk to dry ingredients and mix well.
3. Stir in the shredded cheese and diced ham.
4. Divide the batter evenly among 8 parchment-paper-lined muffin cups.
5. Insert the Drip Tray inside the appliance. Do not insert the Divider.
6. Place the muffin cups on the XL Baking Pan. Slide the Baking Pan into the corresponding shelf position.
7. Use the left Control Knob to select Bake. Set the cooking temperature to 390°F and the cooking time to 10 minutes. Press the Start/Pause Button to begin the cooking cycle, until a toothpick inserted in center of the muffin comes out clean.
8. When the cooking time has completed, transfer the muffins to a plate and serve warm.

Cheesy Mushroom Risotto

PREP TIME: 15 minutes
COOK TIME: 4 hours

8 ounces (227 g) cremini mushrooms, sliced
8 ounces (227 g) shiitake mushrooms, stems removed and sliced
8 ounces (227 g) button mushrooms, sliced
2 cups short-grain brown rice
2 onions, chopped
6 cups vegetable broth
½ cup grated Parmesan cheese
3 tbsps. unsalted butter
5 garlic cloves, minced
1 tsp. dried marjoram leaves

1. Mix the mushrooms, onions, rice, garlic, marjoram, and vegetable broth in a 6-quart casserole dish.
2. Insert the Drip Tray inside the appliance. Do not insert the Divider.
3. Slide the Oven Rack into the corresponding shelf position. Place the casserole dish on the Oven Rack.
4. Use the left Control Knob to select Slow Cook. Set the cooking temperature to 250°F and the cooking time to 4 hours. Press the Start/Pause Button to begin the cooking cycle.
5. With 20 minutes remaining, press the Start/Pause Button, stir in the butter and cheese, and press the Start/Pause Button again to continue cooking.
6. When the cooking time has completed, remove the casserole dish from the airfryer and serve warm.

Healthy Spinach Omelet

PREP TIME: 10 minutes
COOK TIME: 10 minutes

1 tsp. olive oil
¼ cup chopped spinach
3 eggs
1 tbsp. ricotta cheese
1 tbsp. chopped parsley
Salt and ground black pepper, to taste

1. Coat a 7 x 5-inch baking dish with olive oil.
2. In a bowl, beat the eggs with a fork and sprinkle with salt and pepper to taste.
3. Add the spinach, ricotta and parsley. Transfer the mixture into the baking dish.
4. Insert the Drip Tray inside the appliance. Do not insert the Divider.
5. Place the baking dish on the XL Baking Pan. Slide the Baking Pan into the corresponding shelf position.
6. Use the left Control Knob to select Bake. Set the cooking temperature to 330°F and the cooking time to 10 minutes. Press the Start/Pause Button to begin the cooking cycle, until the egg is set.
7. When the cooking time has completed, serve warm.

Nut and Seed Muffins

PREP TIME: 15 minutes
COOK TIME: 14 minutes

Cooking spray
½ cup whole-wheat flour, plus 2 tbsps.
¼ cup oat bran
1 egg
½ cup buttermilk
½ cup grated carrots
¼ cup chopped pecans
¼ cup chopped walnuts
¼ cup brown sugar
2 tbsps. flaxseed meal

½ tsp. baking soda
½ tsp. baking powder
¼ tsp. salt
½ tsp. cinnamon
2 tbsps. melted butter
½ tsp. pure vanilla extract
1 tbsp. pumpkin seeds
1 tbsp. sunflower seeds
Special Equipment:
16 foil muffin cups, paper liners
removed

1. In a large bowl, stir together the flour, bran, flaxseed meal, baking soda, baking powder, sugar, cinnamon and salt.
2. In a medium bowl, beat together the buttermilk, butter, egg, and vanilla. Pour into the flour mixture and stir just until the dry ingredients moisten. Do not beat.
3. Gently stir in carrots, nuts, and seeds.
4. Double up the foil cups so you have 8 total and spray lightly with cooking spray. Divide the batter among the foil cups.
5. Insert the Drip Tray inside the appliance. Do not insert the Divider.
6. Place the foil cups on the XL Baking Pan. Slide the Baking Pan into the corresponding shelf position.
7. Use the left Control Knob to select Bake. Set the cooking temperature to 330°F and the cooking time to 14 minutes. Press the Start/Pause Button to begin the cooking cycle, until a toothpick inserted in center comes out clean
8. When the cooking time has completed, serve warm.

Pepperoni Pita Pizza

PREP TIME: 10 minutes
COOK TIME: 8 minutes

Cooking spray
1 tbsp. pizza sauce
1 pita bread
6 pepperoni slices
¼ cup grated Mozzarella cheese
¼ tsp. garlic powder
¼ tsp. dried oregano

1. Brush the top of the pita bread with the pizza sauce. Put the pepperoni slices over the sauce, followed by the Mozzarella cheese.
2. Season with garlic powder and oregano to taste. Spray with cooking spray.
3. Insert the Drip Tray inside the appliance. Do not insert the Divider.
4. Place the pizza on the Oven Rack. Slide the Oven Rack into the corresponding shelf position.
5. Use the left Control Knob to select Pizza. Set the cooking temperature to 350°F and the cooking time to 8 minutes. Press the Start/ Pause Button to begin the cooking cycle.
6. When the cooking time has completed, serve warm.

Buttermilk Biscuits

PREP TIME: 5 minutes
COOK TIME: 7 minutes

cooking spray
2 cups all-purpose flour, plus more for dusting the work surface
¾ cup buttermilk
6 tbsps. cold unsalted butter, cut into 1-tbsp. slices
1 tbsp. baking powder
¼ tsp. baking soda
2 tsps. sugar
1 tsp. salt

1. In a large mixing bowl, mix the flour, baking powder, baking soda, sugar, and salt and combine well.
2. Using a fork, cut in the butter until the mixture resembles coarse meal.
3. Add the buttermilk and stir until smooth.
4. Dust more flour on a clean work surface. Turn the dough out onto the work surface and roll it out until it is about ½ inch thick.
5. Cut out the biscuits with a 2-inch biscuit cutter.
6. Insert the Drip Tray inside the appliance. Do not insert the Divider.
7. Spray XL Crisper Tray with cooking spray. Place the biscuits on the Crisper Tray and slide the Crisper Tray into the corresponding shelf position.
8. Use the left Control Knob to select Bake. Set the cooking temperature to 360°F and the cooking time to 7 minutes. Press the Start/ Pause Button to begin the cooking cycle.
9. When the cooking time has completed, serve warm.

Homemade Banana Bread

PREP TIME: 10 minutes
COOK TIME: 22 minutes

2 ripe bananas, mashed
1 large egg
1 cup all-purpose flour
1 cup sugar
4 tbsps. (½ stick) unsalted butter, melted
1 tsp. baking soda
1 tsp. salt

1. Spray the insides of 2 mini loaf pans with cooking spray.
2. In a large mixing bowl, mix the mashed bananas and sugar.
3. In a separate large mixing bowl, combine the egg, flour, butter, baking soda, and salt and mix well.
4. Place the banana mixture to the egg and flour mixture and mix well.
5. Divide the batter evenly among the prepared loaf pans.
6. Insert the Drip Tray inside the appliance. Do not insert the Divider.
7. Place the loaf pans on the XL Baking Pan. Slide the Baking Pan into the corresponding shelf position.
8. Use the left Control Knob to select Bake. Set the cooking temperature to 350°F and the cooking time to 22 minutes. Press the Start/Pause Button to begin the cooking cycle. Insert a toothpick into the center of each loaf; if it comes out clean, they are done.
9. When the cooking time has completed, remove the pans from the airfryer. Turn out the loaves onto a wire rack to cool. Serve warm.

Tasty Toasts

PREP TIME: 10 minutes
COOK TIME: 4 slices

4 bread slices
8 ounces ricotta cheese
4 ounces smoked salmon
1 shallot, sliced
1 cup arugula
1 garlic clove, minced
1 tsp. lemon zest
¼ tsp. freshly ground black pepper

1. Insert the Drip Tray inside the appliance. Do not insert the Divider.
2. Place 4 bread slices on the Oven Rack. Slide the Oven Rack into the corresponding shelf position.
3. Use the left Control Knob to select Toast. Set the slices setting to 4 slices and the Darkness setting to Dark. Press the Start/Pause Button to begin the cooking cycle.
4. Meanwhile, put the garlic, ricotta cheese and lemon zest in a food processor and pulse until smooth.
5. When the cooking time has completed, transfer bread slices to a plate.
6. Spread the cheese mixture over each bread slice and top with the salmon, arugula and shallot. Sprinkle with black pepper and serve warm.

Spanish Style Frittata

PREP TIME: 10 minutes COOK TIME: 14 minutes	1 tbsp. olive oil 3 jumbo eggs 1 potato, boiled, peeled and cubed	½ cup frozen corn ½ of chorizo sausage, sliced 2 tbsps. feta cheese, crumbled Salt and black pepper, to taste

1. Grease a 7 x 5-inch baking dish with olive oil.
2. Add the chorizo sausage, corn and cubed potato in the dish.
3. Insert the Drip Tray inside the appliance. Do not insert the Divider.
4. Place the dish on the XL Baking Pan. Slide the Baking Pan into the corresponding shelf position.
5. Use the left Control Knob to select Bake. Set the cooking temperature to 355°F and the cooking time to 14 minutes. Press the Start/Pause Button to begin the cooking cycle.
6. With 6 minutes remaining, press the Start/Pause Button, pour the eggs over the sausage mixture and top with feta cheese, and press the Start/Pause Button again to continue cooking.
7. When the cooking time has completed, serve warm.

Fast Coffee Donuts

PREP TIME: 5 minutes COOK TIME: 8 minutes	cooking spray 1 cup flour ¼ cup coffee ¼ cup sugar	1 tbsp. aquafaba 1 tbsp. sunflower oil ½ tsp. salt 1 tsp. baking powder

1. In a large bowl, combine the sugar, salt, flour, and baking powder.
2. Add the coffee, aquafaba, and sunflower oil and mix until a dough is formed. Leave the dough to rest in and the refrigerator.
3. Remove the dough from the fridge and divide up, kneading each section into a doughnut.
4. Insert the Drip Tray inside the appliance. Do not insert the Divider.
5. Spray XL Crisper Tray with cooking spray. Place the doughnuts on the Crisper Tray and slide the Crisper Tray into the corresponding shelf position.
6. Use the left Control Knob to select Bake. Set the cooking temperature to 400°F and the cooking time to 8 minutes. Press the Start/Pause Button to begin the cooking cycle.
7. When the cooking time has completed, transfer the donuts to a plate. Serve warm.

Gold Avocado

PREP TIME: 5 minutes COOK TIME: 8 minutes	cooking spray 2 large avocados, sliced 2 eggs, beaten 1 cup bread crumbs	½ cup whole wheat flour ¼ tsp. paprika Salt and ground black pepper, to taste

1. Sprinkle the paprika, salt and pepper on the slices of avocado.
2. Lightly coat the avocados with flour. Dredge them in the eggs, before covering with bread crumbs.
3. Insert the Drip Tray inside the appliance. Do not insert the Divider.
4. Use the left Control Knob to select Air Fry. Set the cooking temperature to 400°F and the cooking time to 8 minutes. Set the Shake Indicator and press the Start/Pause Button. Let the appliance preheat.
5. When the appliance has preheated, spray XL Crisper Tray with cooking spray and place the avocados on the Crisper Tray. Slide the Crisper Tray into the corresponding shelf position. Shake avocados halfway through cooking according to the Shake Indicator.
6. When the cooking time has completed, transfer the avocados to a plate. Serve warm.

CHAPTER 3
POULTRY

Crispy Chicken Tenders

PREP TIME: 20 minutes
COOK TIME: 24 minutes

cooking spray
2 (6-ounces) boneless, skinless chicken breasts, pounded into ½-inch thickness and cut into tenders
2 large eggs
1½ cups panko breadcrumbs
¾ cup buttermilk
½ cup all-purpose flour
¼ cup Parmesan cheese, finely grated
1½ tsps. Worcestershire sauce, divided
½ tsp. smoked paprika, divided
Salt and ground black pepper, as required

1. Mix the buttermilk, ¾ tsp. of Worcestershire sauce, ¼ tsp. of paprika, salt, and black pepper in a bowl.
2. Combine the flour, remaining paprika, salt, and black pepper in another bowl.
3. Whisk the egg and remaining Worcestershire sauce in a third bowl.
4. Mix the breadcrumbs and Parmesan cheese in a fourth bowl.
5. Put the chicken tenders into the buttermilk mixture and refrigerate overnight.
6. Remove the chicken tenders from the buttermilk mixture and dredge into the flour mixture.
7. Then dip into the egg and coat with the breadcrumb mixture.
8. Insert the Drip Tray inside the appliance. Do not insert the Divider.
9. Use the left Control Knob to select Air Fry. Set the cooking temperature to 390°F and the cooking time to 24 minutes. Set the Shake Indicator and press the Start/Pause Button. Let the appliance preheat.
10. When the appliance has preheated, spray XL Crisper Tray with cooking spray and place the chicken tenders in a single layer on the Crisper Tray. Slide the Crisper Tray into the corresponding shelf position. Shake chicken tenders halfway through cooking according to the Shake Indicator.
11. When the cooking time has completed, transfer the chicken tenders to a plate. Serve warm.

BBQ Chicken Wings

PREP TIME: 10 minutes
COOK TIME: 25 minutes

2 pounds chicken wings, cut into drumettes and flats
½ cup BBQ sauce

1. Insert the Drip Tray inside the appliance. Do not insert the Divider.
2. Place the chicken wings on the XL Grill Plate. Slide the Grill Plate into the corresponding shelf position.
3. Use the left Control Knob to select Grill. Set the cooking temperature to 400°F and the cooking time to 25 minutes. Press the Start/Pause Button to begin the cooking cycle, flipping halfway through cooking.
4. When the cooking time has completed, transfer the chicken wings to a plate. Drizzle with the BBQ sauce to serve.

Chinese Chicken Drumsticks

SERVES 4

PREP TIME: 15 minutes
COOK TIME: 22 minutes

½ tsp. sesame oil
4 (6-ounces) chicken drumsticks
1 tbsp. oyster sauce
1 tsp. Chinese five spice powder
1 tsp. light soy sauce
Salt and white pepper, as required

1. Mix the sauces, sesame oil, five spice powder, salt, and black pepper in a bowl.
2. Rub the chicken drumsticks with this marinade and refrigerate for about 40 minutes.
3. Insert the Drip Tray inside the appliance. Do not insert the Divider.
4. Place the chicken drumsticks on the XL Baking Pan. Slide the Baking Pan into the corresponding shelf position.
5. Use the left Control Knob to select Roast. Set the cooking temperature to 390°F and the cooking time to 22 minutes. Press the Start/Pause Button to begin the cooking cycle, flipping halfway through cooking.
6. When the cooking time has completed, transfer the chicken drumsticks to a plate. Serve warm.

Chicken and Tomato Kabobs

SERVES 3

PREP TIME: 20 minutes
COOK TIME: 25 minutes

1 tbsp. olive oil
1 lb. skinless, boneless chicken thighs, cut into cubes
1 large red onion, cut into large chunks
2 small tomatoes, seeded and cut into large chunks
½ cup plain Greek yogurt
Wooden skewers, presoaked
2 tsps. curry powder
½ tsp. smoked paprika
¼ tsp. cayenne pepper
Salt, to taste

1. Mix the chicken cubes, olive oil, yogurt, and spices in a large baking dish.
2. Thread the chicken, tomatoes and onion onto presoaked wooden skewers.
3. Coat the skewers generously with the marinade and refrigerate for about 3 hours.
4. Insert the Drip Tray inside the appliance. Do not insert the Divider.
5. Place the skewers on the XL Baking Pan. Slide the Baking Pan into the corresponding shelf position.
6. Use the left Control Knob to select Roast. Set the cooking temperature to 360°F and the cooking time to 25 minutes. Press the Start/Pause Button to begin the cooking cycle, flipping halfway through cooking.
7. When the cooking time has completed, transfer the skewers to a plate. Serve warm.

Bacon Wrapped Chicken Breasts

SERVES 4

PREP TIME: 20 minutes
COOK TIME: 28 minutes

2 (8-ounces) chicken breasts, cut each breast in half horizontally
12 bacon strips
6-7 fresh basil leaves
2 tbsps. water
2 tbsps. fish sauce
1 tbsp. palm sugar
1½ tsps. honey
Salt and ground black pepper, as required

1. Cook the palm sugar in a small heavy-bottomed pan over medium-low heat for about 3 minutes until caramelized.
2. Stir in the basil, fish sauce and water and transfer to a bowl.
3. Season each chicken breast with salt and black pepper and coat with the palm sugar mixture.
4. Refrigerate to marinate for about 6 hours and wrap each chicken piece with 3 bacon strips. Then dip into the honey.
5. Insert the Drip Tray inside the appliance. Do not insert the Divider.
6. Place the chicken breasts on the XL Grill Plate. Slide the Grill Plate into the corresponding shelf position.
7. Use the left Control Knob to select Grill. Set the cooking temperature to 390°F and the cooking time to 25 minutes. Press the Start/Pause Button to begin the cooking cycle, flipping halfway through cooking.
8. When the cooking time has completed, transfer the chicken breasts to a plate. Serve warm.

Chicken Slices with Broccoli

SERVES 3

PREP TIME: 20 minutes
COOK TIME: 18 minutes

cooking spray
1 pound boneless, skinless chicken breasts, sliced
1½ cups small broccoli florets
1/6 cup butter
1½ tbsps. dried parsley, crushed
½ tbsp. garlic powder
½ tbsp. onion powder
¼ tsp. paprika
¼ tsp. red chili powder

1. Mix the butter, parsley and spices in a small bowl.
2. Coat the chicken slices and broccoli generously with the spice mixture.
3. Insert the Drip Tray inside the appliance. Insert the Divider.
4. Use the left Control Knob to select Air Fry. Set the cooking temperature to 390°F and the cooking time to 18 minutes. Use the right Control Knob to select Roast. Set the cooking temperature to 390°F and the cooking time to 15 minutes. Press the Sync Button and the Start/Pause Button. Let the left zone preheat.
5. When preheat is completed, spray Crisper Tray with cooking spray and place the marinated chicken slices on the Crisper Tray. Slide the Crisper Tray into the corresponding shelf position on the left. Place the broccoli on the Baking Pan. Slide the Baking Pan into the corresponding shelf position on the right. Shake foods in both zones halfway through cooking.
6. When the cooking time has completed, serve the chicken with broccoli.

Lemon-Rosemary Roasted Chicken

SERVES 6 TO 8

PREP TIME: 20 minutes COOK TIME: 50 minutes	½ cup (120 ml) extra-virgin olive oil, divided 1 (3- to 4-pound, 1.4 to 1.8 kg) roasting chicken 8 garlic cloves, roughly chopped 2 lemons, thinly sliced 2 to 4 tbsps. chopped fresh rosemary 2 tsps. salt, divided 1 tsp. freshly ground black pepper, divided

1. Put the whole chicken breast-side down on a large work surface. Cut along the backbone with a very sharp knife, starting at the tail end and up to the neck. Pull apart the two sides, opening up the chicken. Flip it over, breast-side up, pressing down with your hands to flatten the chicken.
2. Loosen the skin over the breasts and thighs by cutting a small incision and sticking fingers inside to pull the skin away from the meat without removing it.
3. In a small bowl, combine the garlic, ¼ cup olive oil, 1 tsp. salt, rosemary, and ½ tsp. pepper and whisk together.
4. Rub the oil mixture evenly under the skin of each breast and each thigh. Add the lemon slices evenly.
5. Whisk together the remaining oil, ½ tsp. pepper and 1 tsp. salt, and rub over the outside of the chicken.
6. Insert the Drip Tray inside the appliance. Do not insert the Divider.
7. Truss the chicken. Slide the chicken onto the Rotisserie Shaft and secure the chicken with the Rotisserie Forks. Secure the Rotisserie Shaft in the appliance.
8. Use the left Control Knob to select Rotisserie. Set the cooking temperature to 375°F and the cooking time to 50 minutes. Press the Start/Pause Button to begin the cooking cycle. Cook the chicken until the chicken is cooked through and an instant-read thermometer inserted into the thickest part of chicken registers 165°F.
9. When the cooking time has completed, let the chicken rest for 20 minutes before serving.

Chicken with Veggies

SERVES 2

PREP TIME: 20 minutes COOK TIME: 24 minutes	2 tbsps. olive oil 2 skinless, boneless chicken breasts 4 small artichoke hearts, quartered 4 fresh large button mushrooms, quartered ½ small onion, cut in large chunks 2 garlic cloves, minced 2 tbsps. fresh parsley, chopped 2 tbsps. chicken broth 2 tbsps. red wine vinegar 1 tbsp. Dijon mustard ⅛ tsp. dried thyme ⅛ tsp. dried basil Salt and black pepper, as required

1. Mix the garlic, broth, vinegar, olive oil, mustard, thyme, and basil in a bowl.
2. Mix the artichokes, mushrooms, onions, salt, and black pepper in another bowl.
3. Insert the Drip Tray inside the appliance. Insert the Divider.
4. Place the chicken breasts on the Grill Plate and spread half of the mustard mixture evenly. Slide the Grill Plate into the corresponding shelf position on the left. Place the vegetables on the Baking Pan. Slide the Baking Pan into the corresponding shelf position on the right.
5. Use the left Control Knob to select Grill. Set the cooking temperature to 400°F and the cooking time to 24 minutes. Use the right Control Knob to select Roast. Set the cooking temperature to 390°F and the cooking time to 18 minutes. Press the Sync Button and the Start/Pause Button to begin the cooking cycle. Halfway through cooking, coat the chicken breasts with the remaining mustard mixture and flip the side.
6. When the cooking time has completed, transfer the chicken and vegetables to a plate. Serve garnished with parsley.

Cornish Game Hen

PREP TIME: 20 minutes COOK TIME: 30 minutes	½ cup olive oil 2 pounds Cornish game hen, backbone removed and halved 1 tsp. fresh lemon zest, finely grated	1 tsp. fresh rosemary, chopped 1 tsp. fresh thyme, chopped ¼ tsp. sugar ¼ tsp. red pepper flakes, crushed Salt and black pepper, to taste

1. Mix the olive oil, lemon zest, herbs, sugar, and spices in a medium bowl.
2. Stir in the Cornish game hen and refrigerate to marinate well for about 24 hours.
3. Insert the Drip Tray inside the appliance. Do not insert the Divider.
4. Truss the Cornish game hen. Slide the Cornish game hen onto the Rotisserie Shaft and secure the Cornish game hen with the Rotisserie Forks. Secure the Rotisserie Shaft in the appliance.
5. Use the left Control Knob to select Rotisserie. Set the cooking temperature to 390°F and the cooking time to 30 minutes. Press the Start/Pause Button to begin the cooking cycle.
6. When the cooking time has completed, transfer the Cornish game hen to a plate and serve warm.

Sweet and Sour Chicken Thighs

PREP TIME: 15 minutes COOK TIME: 20 minutes	2 (4-ounces) skinless, boneless chicken thighs ½ cup corn flour 1 scallion, finely chopped 1 garlic clove, minced	½ tbsp. rice vinegar ½ tbsp. soy sauce 1 tsp. sugar Salt and black pepper, as required

1. Mix all the ingredients except chicken thighs and corn flour in a bowl.
2. Place the corn flour in another bowl.
3. Coat the chicken thighs into the marinade and then dredge into the corn flour.
4. Insert the Drip Tray inside the appliance. Do not insert the Divider.
5. Use the left Control Knob to select Air Fry. Set the cooking temperature to 390°F and the cooking time to 20 minutes. Set the Shake Indicator and press the Start/Pause Button. Let the appliance preheat.
6. When the appliance has preheated, spray XL Crisper Tray with cooking spray and place the chicken thighs on the Crisper Tray. Slide the Crisper Tray into the corresponding shelf position. Halfway through cooking, flip the chicken thighs over according to the Shake Indicator.
7. When the cooking time has completed, transfer the chicken thighs to a plate. Serve warm.

Appetizing Chicken Pieces

PREP TIME: 30 minutes COOK TIME: 18 minutes	cooking spray ½ tbsp. olive oil ¾ pound chicken pieces 1 lemon, cut into wedges 3 tbsps. coconut sugar	1 tbsp. fresh rosemary, chopped 1 tsp. ginger, minced 1 tbsp. soy sauce 1 tbsp. oyster sauce

1. Mix the chicken pieces, ginger, soy sauce and olive oil in a bowl.
2. Marinate and refrigerate for about 30 minutes.
3. Insert the Drip Tray inside the appliance. Do not insert the Divider.
4. Use the left Control Knob to select Air Fry. Set the cooking temperature to 390°F and the cooking time to 18 minutes. Press the Start/Pause Button. Let the appliance preheat.
5. When the appliance has preheated, spray XL Crisper Tray with cooking spray and place the chicken on the Crisper Tray. Slide the Crisper Tray into the corresponding shelf position.
6. Meanwhile, mix the remaining ingredients in a small bowl.
7. With 10 minutes remaining, press the Start/Pause Button and spread the sauce over the chicken. Squeeze juice from lemon wedges over chicken and top with the wedges. Press the Start/Pause Button again to continue cooking.
8. When the cooking time has completed, transfer the chicken to a plate. Serve warm.

CHAPTER 4
VEGETABLES

Honey Beets and Onions

PREP TIME: 14 minutes
COOK TIME: 6 hours

2 tbsps. melted coconut oil
10 medium beets, peeled and sliced
3 red onions, chopped
1 cup water
⅓ cup lemon juice
⅓ cup honey
4 garlic cloves, minced
3 tbsps. cornstarch
½ tsp. salt

1. Mix the beets, onions, and garlic in a 6-quart baking dish.
2. Combine the coconut oil, honey, lemon juice, water, cornstarch, and salt in a medium bowl, until well mixed. Pour this mixture over the beets.
3. Insert the Drip Tray inside the appliance. Do not insert the Divider.
4. Slide the Oven Rack into the corresponding shelf position. Place the baking dish on the Oven Rack.
5. Use the left Control Knob to select Slow Cook. Set the cooking temperature to 250°F and the cooking time to 6 hours. Press the Start/Pause Button to begin the cooking cycle, until the beets are soft and the sauce has thickened.
6. When the cooking time has completed, serve warm.

Breadcrumbs Stuffed Mushrooms

PREP TIME: 15 minutes
COOK TIME: 15 minutes

1½ tbsps. olive oil
16 small button mushrooms, stemmed and gills removed
1½ spelt bread slices
1 tbsp. flat-leaf parsley, finely chopped
1 garlic clove, crushed
Salt and black pepper, to taste

1. Add the bread slices in a food processor and pulse until fine crumbs form.
2. Transfer the crumbs into a bowl and stir in the oil, garlic, parsley, salt and black pepper.
3. Gently stuff the breadcrumbs mixture in each mushroom cap.
4. Insert the Drip Tray inside the appliance. Do not insert the Divider.
5. Use the left Control Knob to select Air Fry. Set the cooking temperature to 390°F and the cooking time to 15 minutes. Press the Start/Pause Button. Let the appliance preheat.
6. When the appliance has preheated, place the mushroom caps in a single layer on the XL Crisper Tray. Slide the Crisper Tray into the corresponding shelf position.
7. When the cooking time has completed, transfer the mushroom caps to a plate and serve warm.

Red Bell Peppers Cups

PREP TIME: 10 minutes
COOK TIME: 15 minutes

cooking spray
8 mini red bell peppers, tops and seeds removed
¾ cup feta cheese, crumbled
1 tsp. fresh parsley, chopped
½ tbsp. olive oil
Freshly ground black pepper, to taste

1. Mix the feta cheese, parsley, olive oil and black pepper in a small bowl.
2. Stuff the red bell peppers with the feta mixture.
3. Insert the Drip Tray inside the appliance. Do not insert the Divider.
4. Use the left Control Knob to select Air Fry. Set the cooking temperature to 390°F and the cooking time to 15 minutes. Press the Start/Pause Button. Let the appliance preheat.
5. When the appliance has preheated, spray XL Crisper Tray with cooking spray and place the bell peppers in a single layer on the Crisper Tray. Slide the Crisper Tray into the corresponding shelf position.
6. When the cooking time has completed, transfer the bell peppers to a plate. Serve warm.

Garden Veggie Medley

PREP TIME: 10 minutes
COOK TIME: 25 minutes

1 tbsp. olive oil
2 yellow bell peppers, seeded and chopped
3 tomatoes, chopped
1 zucchini, chopped
1 eggplant, chopped
2 small onions, chopped
2 garlic cloves, minced
2 tbsps. herbs de Provence
1 tbsp. balsamic vinegar
Salt and black pepper, to taste

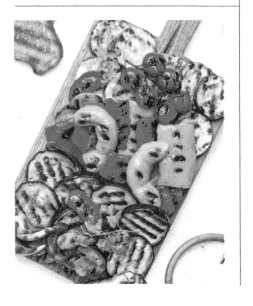

1. Mix all the ingredients in a large bowl and toss to coat well.
2. Insert the Drip Tray inside the appliance. Do not insert the Divider.
3. Place the vegetables in a single layer on the XL Grill Plate. Slide the Grill Plate into the corresponding shelf position.
4. Use the left Control Knob to select Grill. Set the cooking temperature to 390°F and the cooking time to 25 minutes. Press the Start/Pause Button to begin the cooking cycle, flipping halfway through cooking.
5. When the cooking time has completed, transfer the vegetables to a plate and serve warm.

Buttered Broccoli

PREP TIME: 10 minutes
COOK TIME: 10 minutes

2 tbsps. butter, melted
4 cups fresh broccoli florets
Salt and black pepper, to taste

1. Mix the broccoli, butter, salt, and black pepper in a bowl and toss to coat well.
2. Insert the Drip Tray inside the appliance. Do not insert the Divider.
3. Use the left Control Knob to select Air Fry. Set the cooking temperature to 390°F and the cooking time to 10 minutes. Set the Shake Indicator and press the Start/Pause Button. Let the appliance preheat.
4. When the appliance has preheated, spray XL Crisper Tray with cooking spray and place the broccoli florets on the Crisper Tray. Slide the Crisper Tray into the corresponding shelf position. Shake broccoli florets halfway through cooking according to the Shake Indicator.
5. When the cooking time has completed, transfer the broccoli florets to a plate. Serve warm.

Asparagus with Parmesan

PREP TIME: 15 minutes
COOK TIME: 22 minutes

1 tbsp. butter, melted
1 pound fresh asparagus, trimmed
1 tbsp. Parmesan cheese, grated
1 tsp. garlic powder
Salt and black pepper, to taste

1. Mix the asparagus, Parmesan cheese, butter, garlic powder, salt, and black pepper in a medium bowl and toss to coat well.
2. Insert the Drip Tray inside the appliance. Do not insert the Divider.
3. Place the asparagus on the XL Baking Pan. Slide the Baking Pan into the corresponding shelf position.
4. Use the left Control Knob to select Roast. Set the cooking temperature to 390°F and the cooking time to 22 minutes. Press the Start/Pause Button to begin the cooking cycle, flipping halfway through cooking.
5. When the cooking time has completed, transfer the asparagus to a plate and serve warm.

Smashed Potatoes with Thyme

SERVES 12

PREP TIME: 18 minutes
COOK TIME: 6 hours

3 tbsps. olive oil
3½ pounds (1.6 kg) red or creamer potatoes, rinsed
2 onions, minced
12 garlic cloves, peeled and sliced
⅓ cup grated Parmesan cheese
½ cup vegetable broth
1 tsp. dried dill leaves
1 tsp. dried thyme leaves
½ tsp. salt

1. Mix the potatoes, onions, garlic, olive oil, vegetable broth, thyme, dill and salt in a 6-quart baking dish.
2. Insert the Drip Tray inside the appliance. Do not insert the Divider.
3. Slide the Oven Rack into the corresponding shelf position. Place the baking dish on the Oven Rack.
4. Use the left Control Knob to select Slow Cook. Set the cooking temperature to 250°F and the cooking time to 6 hours. Press the Start/Pause Button to begin the cooking cycle, until the potatoes are soft.
5. When the cooking time has completed, mash the potatoes with a potato masher in the baking dish, leaving some chunky pieces. Toss in the Parmesan cheese and serve hot.

Green Beans and Mushroom

SERVES 6

PREP TIME: 15 minutes
COOK TIME: 15 minutes

cooking spray
3 tbsps. olive oil
24 ounces fresh green beans, trimmed
2 cups fresh button mushrooms, sliced
2 tbsps. fresh lemon juice
1 tsp. ground sage
1 tsp. garlic powder
1 tsp. onion powder
Salt and black pepper, to taste

1. Mix the oil, lemon juice, sage, and spices in a bowl and divide among two parts.
2. Put the green beans in a medium bowl with half of the herb mixture and toss to coat well. Repeat with the mushrooms.
3. Insert the Drip Tray inside the appliance. Insert the Divider.
4. Use the left Control Knob to select Air Fry. Set the cooking temperature to 390°F and the cooking time to 15 minutes. Use the right Control Knob to select Roast. Set the cooking temperature to 390°F and the cooking time to 12 minutes. Press the Sync Button and the Start/Pause Button. Let the left zone preheat.
5. When preheat is completed, spray Crisper Tray with cooking spray and place the green beans on the Crisper Tray. Slide the Crisper Tray into the corresponding shelf position on the left. Place the mushrooms on the Baking Pan. Slide the Baking Pan into the corresponding shelf position on the right. Shake foods in both zones halfway through cooking.
6. When the cooking time has completed, serve green beans with mushrooms.

Maple Glazed Parsnips

PREP TIME: 10 minutes COOK TIME: 35 minutes	1 tbsp. butter, melted 2 pounds parsnips, peeled and cut into 1-inch chunks 1 tbsp. dried parsley flakes, crushed 2 tbsps. maple syrup ¼ tsp. red pepper flakes, crushed

1. Mix the parsnips and butter in a large bowl and toss to coat well.
2. Insert the Drip Tray inside the appliance. Do not insert the Divider.
3. Place the parsnips on the XL Baking Pan. Slide the Baking Pan into the corresponding shelf position.
4. Use the left Control Knob to select Roast. Set the cooking temperature to 390°F and the cooking time to 35 minutes. Press the Start/Pause Button to begin the cooking cycle, flipping halfway through cooking.
5. Meanwhile, mix the remaining ingredients in a small bowl.
6. With 5 minutes remaining, press the Start/Pause Button, spread the mixture over parsnips and press the Start/Pause Button again to continue cooking.
7. When the cooking time has completed, transfer the parsnips to a plate and serve warm.

Lemony Green Beans

PREP TIME: 15 minutes COOK TIME: 10 minutes	cooking spray 1 tsp. unsalted butter, melted 1 pound green beans, trimmed and halved 1 tbsp. fresh lemon juice ¼ tsp. garlic powder

1. Mix all the ingredients in a medium bowl and toss to coat well.
2. Insert the Drip Tray inside the appliance. Do not insert the Divider.
3. Use the left Control Knob to select Air Fry. Set the cooking temperature to 390°F and the cooking time to 10 minutes. Set the Shake Indicator and press the Start/Pause Button. Let the appliance preheat.
4. When the appliance has preheated, spray XL Crisper Tray with cooking spray and place the green beans on the Crisper Tray. Slide the Crisper Tray into the corresponding shelf position. Shake green beans halfway through cooking according to the Shake Indicator.
5. When the cooking time has completed, transfer the green beans to a plate. Serve warm.

Cheesy Brussels Sprouts

PREP TIME: 15 minutes COOK TIME: 15 minutes	cooking spray 1 tbsp. extra-virgin olive oil 1 pound Brussels sprouts, trimmed and halved ¼ cup Parmesan cheese, shredded ¼ cup whole wheat breadcrumbs 1 tbsp. balsamic vinegar Salt and black pepper, to taste

1. Mix the Brussels sprouts, vinegar, oil, salt, and black pepper in a medium bowl and toss to coat well.
2. Insert the Drip Tray inside the appliance. Do not insert the Divider.
3. Use the left Control Knob to select Air Fry. Set the cooking temperature to 400°F and the cooking time to 15 minutes. Set the Shake Indicator and press the Start/Pause Button. Let the appliance preheat.
4. When the appliance has preheated, spray XL Crisper Tray with cooking spray and place the Brussels sprouts on the Crisper Tray. Slide the Crisper Tray into the corresponding shelf position. Shake Brussels sprouts halfway through cooking according to the Shake Indicator.
5. With 5 minutes remaining, press the Start/Pause Button, sprinkle with breadcrumbs and cheese, and press the Start/Pause Button again to continue cooking.
6. When the cooking time has completed, transfer the Brussels sprouts to a plate. Serve warm.

CHAPTER 5
BEEF

Tasty London Broil

PREP TIME: 15 minutes
COOK TIME: 30 minutes

2 tbsps. olive oil
2 pounds (907 g) London broil
3 large garlic cloves, minced
3 tbsps. whole-grain mustard
3 tbsps. balsamic vinegar
½ tsp. dried hot red pepper flakes
Sea salt and ground black pepper, to taste

1. Wash and dry the London broil. Score its sides with a knife.
2. Mix the remaining ingredients in a small bowl. Rub this mixture into the broil, coating it well. Let marinate for a minimum of 3 hours.
3. Insert the Drip Tray inside the appliance. Do not insert the Divider.
4. Slide the London broil onto the Rotisserie Shaft and secure the London broil with the Rotisserie Forks. Secure the Rotisserie Shaft in the appliance.
5. Use the left Control Knob to select Rotisserie. Set the cooking temperature to 375°F and the cooking time to 30 minutes. Press the Start/Pause Button to begin the cooking cycle.
6. After 25 minutes, start checking the internal temperature with an instant-read thermometer inserted into the thickest part of the meat. Cook until the desired doneness is reached.
7. When the cooking time has completed, let the beef rest for 10 minutes and cut into desired size slices to serve.

Herbed Beef Roast

PREP TIME: 10 minutes
COOK TIME: 40 minutes

2 pounds beef roast
1 tbsp. olive oil
1 tsp. dried rosemary, crushed
1 tsp. dried thyme, crushed
Salt, to taste

1. Rub the roast generously with herb mixture and coat evenly with olive oil.
2. Insert the Drip Tray inside the appliance. Do not insert the Divider.
3. Slide the roast onto the Rotisserie Shaft and secure the roast with the Rotisserie Forks. Secure the Rotisserie Shaft in the appliance.
4. Use the left Control Knob to select Rotisserie. Set the cooking temperature to 390°F and the cooking time to 40 minutes. Press the Start/Pause Button to begin the cooking cycle.
5. After 35 minutes, start checking the internal temperature with an instant-read thermometer inserted into the thickest part of the roast. Cook until the desired doneness is reached.
6. When the cooking time has completed, transfer the roast to a plate. Cut into desired size slices and serve warm.

Buttered Rib Eye Steak

PREP TIME: 20 minutes
COOK TIME: 15 minutes

½ cup unsalted butter, softened
2 tbsps. fresh parsley, chopped
2 (8-ounces) rib eye steaks
2 tsps. garlic, minced
1 tsp. Worcestershire sauce
1 tbsp. olive oil
Salt and black pepper, to taste

1. Mix the butter, garlic, parsley, Worcestershire sauce, and salt in a small bowl.
2. Place the butter mixture onto a parchment paper, roll into a log and refrigerate for about 3 hours.
3. Rub the steak generously with olive oil, salt and black pepper.
4. Insert the Drip Tray inside the appliance. Do not insert the Divider.
5. Place the steaks on the XL Baking Pan. Slide the Baking Pan into the corresponding shelf position.
6. Use the left Control Knob to select Roast. Set the cooking temperature to 390°F and the cooking time to 15 minutes. Press the Start/Pause Button to begin the cooking cycle, flipping halfway through cooking.
7. When the cooking time has completed, transfer the steaks to a plate and cut into desired size slices. Cut the butter log into slices and top over the steak to serve.

Beef and Veggie Kebabs

PREP TIME: 20 minutes
COOK TIME: 16 minutes

¼ cup olive oil
1 pound sirloin steak, cut into 1-inch chunks
8 ounces baby Bella mushrooms, stems removed
1 red onion, cut into 1-inch pieces
1 large bell pepper, seeded and cut into 1-inch pieces

¼ cup soy sauce
1 tbsp. garlic, minced
1 tsp. coconut sugar
½ tsp. ground cumin
Salt and black pepper, to taste

1. Mix the soy sauce, oil, garlic, coconut sugar, cumin, salt, and black pepper in a large bowl.
2. Coat the steak cubes generously with marinade and refrigerate to marinate for about 30 minutes.
3. Thread the steak cubes, mushrooms, bell pepper and onion onto metal skewers.
4. Insert the Drip Tray inside the appliance. Do not insert the Divider.
5. Use the left Control Knob to select Air Fry. Set the cooking temperature to 390°F and the cooking time to 16 minutes. Set the Shake Indicator and press the Start/Pause Button. Let the appliance preheat.
6. When the appliance has preheated, place the skewers in a single layer on the XL Crisper Tray. Slide the Crisper Tray into the corresponding shelf position. Halfway through cooking, flip the skewers over according to the Shake Indicator.
7. When the cooking time has completed, transfer the skewers to a plate and serve warm.

Grilled Beef Burgers

PREP TIME: 20 minutes
COOK TIME: 16 minutes

2 pounds ground beef
12 cheddar cheese slices
12 dinner rolls
6 tbsps. tomato ketchup
Salt and black pepper, to taste

1. Mix the beef, salt and black pepper in a large bowl.
2. Shape this beef mixture into 6 equal-sized patties.
3. Insert the Drip Tray inside the appliance. Do not insert the Divider.
4. Place the patties in a single layer on the XL Grill Plate. Slide the Grill Plate into the corresponding shelf position.
5. Use the left Control Knob to select Grill. Set the cooking temperature to 390°F and the cooking time to 16 minutes. Press the Start/Pause Button to begin the cooking cycle, flipping halfway through cooking.
6. When the cooking time has completed, transfer the patties to a plate. Top each patty with 1 cheese slice. Arrange the patties between rolls and drizzle with ketchup. Serve hot.

Spicy Beef Jerky

PREP TIME: 20 minutes
COOK TIME: 5 hours

1 pound bottom round beef, cut into thin strips
½ cup soy sauce
½ cup dark brown sugar
¼ cup Worcestershire sauce
1 tbsp. chili pepper sauce
1 tbsp. hickory liquid smoke
1 tsp. onion powder
1 tsp. garlic powder
1 tsp. cayenne pepper
½ tsp. smoked paprika
½ tsp. ground black pepper

1. Mix the brown sugar, sauces, liquid smoke, and spices in a bowl.
2. Coat the beef strips with this marinade generously and marinate overnight.
3. Insert the Drip Tray inside the appliance. Do not insert the Divider.
4. Place the beef strips in a single layer on the XL Crisper Tray. Slide the Crisper Tray into the corresponding shelf position.
5. Use the left Control Knob to select Dehydrate. Set the cooking temperature to 150°F and the cooking time to 5 hours. Press the Start/Pause Button to begin the cooking cycle.
6. When the cooking time has completed, transfer the beef strips to a plate. Serve warm.

Bacon Wrapped Filet Mignon

PREP TIME: 15 minutes
COOK TIME: 15 minutes

1 tsp. avocado oil
2 bacon slices
2 (6-ounces) filet mignon steaks
Salt and black pepper, to taste

1. Wrap each mignon steak with 1 bacon slice and secure with a toothpick.
2. Sprinkle the steaks generously with salt and black pepper and spread with avocado oil.
3. Insert the Drip Tray inside the appliance. Do not insert the Divider.
4. Place the steaks on the XL Grill Plate. Slide the Grill Plate into the corresponding shelf position.
5. Use the left Control Knob to select Grill. Set the cooking temperature to 375°F and the cooking time to 15 minutes. Press the Start/Pause Button to begin the cooking cycle, flipping halfway through cooking.
6. When the cooking time has completed, transfer the steaks to a plate and cut into desired size slices to serve.

Beef Chuck with Brussels Sprouts

PREP TIME: 20 minutes
COOK TIME: 25 minutes

cooking spray
1 pound (454 g) beef chuck shoulder steak
2 tbsps. vegetable oil
1 tbsp. red wine vinegar
1 tsp. fine sea salt
½ tsp. ground black pepper
1 tsp. smoked paprika
1 tsp. onion powder
½ tsp. garlic powder
½ pound (227 g) Brussels sprouts, cleaned and halved
½ tsp. fennel seeds
1 tsp. dried basil
1 tsp. dried sage

1. Massage the beef with the vegetable oil, wine vinegar, salt, black pepper, paprika, onion powder, and garlic powder, coating it well. Let marinate for a minimum of 3 hours.
2. Insert the Drip Tray inside the appliance. Insert the Divider.
3. Use the left Control Knob to select Air Fry. Set the cooking temperature to 400°F and the cooking time to 25 minutes. Use the right Control Knob to select Roast. Set the cooking temperature to 390°F and the cooking time to 20 minutes. Press the Sync Button and the Start/Pause Button. Let the left zone preheat.
4. When preheat is completed, spray Crisper Tray with cooking spray and place the Brussels sprouts on the Crisper Tray. Slide the Crisper Tray into the corresponding shelf position on the left. Remove the beef from the marinade and put on the Baking Pan. Slide the Baking Pan into the corresponding shelf position on the right. Halfway through cooking, shake Brussels sprouts for 10 seconds and flip the beef over.
5. When the cooking time has completed, serve beef with Brussels sprouts.

Beef Bratwursts

PREP TIME: 5 minutes COOK TIME: 15 minutes	cooking spray 4 (3-ounce / 85-g) beef bratwursts

1. Insert the Drip Tray inside the appliance. Do not insert the Divider.
2. Use the left Control Knob to select Air Fry. Set the cooking temperature to 375°F and the cooking time to 15 minutes. Set the Shake Indicator and press the Start/Pause Button. Let the appliance preheat.
3. When the appliance has preheated, spray XL Crisper Tray with cooking spray and place the beef bratwursts on the Crisper Tray. Slide the Crisper Tray into the corresponding shelf position. Halfway through cooking, flip the beef bratwursts over according to the Shake Indicator.
4. When the cooking time has completed, transfer the beef bratwursts to a plate. Serve hot.

Beef Loin with Thyme and Parsley

PREP TIME: 5 minutes COOK TIME: 15 minutes	1 tbsp. butter, melted 1 pound (454 g) beef loin ¼ tsp. dried thyme ¼ tsp. dried parsley 1 tsp. garlic salt

1. In a small bowl, combine the melted butter, thyme, garlic salt, and parsley.
2. Cut the beef loin into slices and generously apply the seasoned butter with a brush.
3. Insert the Drip Tray inside the appliance. Do not insert the Divider.
4. Place the beef loin on the XL Baking Pan. Slide the Baking Pan into the corresponding shelf position.
5. Use the left Control Knob to select Roast. Set the cooking temperature to 390°F and the cooking time to 15 minutes. Press the Start/Pause Button to begin the cooking cycle, flipping halfway through cooking.
6. When the cooking time has completed, transfer the beef slices to a plate. Serve warm.

Steak with Bell Peppers

PREP TIME: 20 minutes COOK TIME: 18 minutes	2 tbsps. olive oil 1¼ pounds beef steak, cut into thin strips 2 green bell peppers, seeded and cubed 1 red bell pepper, seeded and cubed 1 red onion, sliced	1 tsp. dried oregano, crushed 1 tsp. onion powder 1 tsp. garlic powder 1 tsp. red chili powder 1 tsp. paprika Salt, to taste

1. Mix the oregano and spices in a bowl.
2. Add the bell peppers, onion, oil, and beef strips and mix until well combined.
3. Insert the Drip Tray inside the appliance. Insert the Divider.
4. Place the beef strips on the Baking Pan. Slide the Baking Pan into the corresponding shelf position on the left.
5. Use the left Control Knob to select Roast. Set the cooking temperature to 390°F and the cooking time to 18 minutes. Use the right Control Knob to select Air Fry. Set the cooking temperature to 390°F and the cooking time to 15 minutes. Press the Sync Button and the Start/Pause Button to begin the cooking cycle.
6. When the cooking timers of both cooking zones synchronize, press the Start/Pause Button and pace the vegetables on the Crisper Tray. Slide the Crisper Tray into the corresponding shelf position on the right. Press the Start/Pause Button again to continue cooking. Shake foods in both zones halfway through cooking.
7. When the cooking time has completed, serve beef strips with vegetables.

CHAPTER 6
FISH AND SEAFOOD

Chili Shrimps

PREP TIME: 15 minutes
COOK TIME: 8 minutes

2 tbsps. olive oil
1 pound shrimps, peeled and deveined
1 tsp. old bay seasoning
½ tsp. smoked paprika
½ tsp. red chili flakes
½ tsp. cayenne pepper
Salt, as required

1. Mix the shrimps with olive oil and other seasonings in a large bowl.
2. Insert the Drip Tray inside the appliance. Do not insert the Divider.
3. Place the shrimps on the XL Grill Plate. Slide the Grill Plate into the corresponding shelf position.
4. Use the left Control Knob to select Grill. Set the cooking temperature to 390°F and the cooking time to 8 minutes. Press the Start/Pause Button to begin the cooking cycle, shaking halfway through cooking.
5. When the cooking time has completed, transfer the shrimps to a plate. Serve warm.

Buttered Scallops

PREP TIME: 10 minutes
COOK TIME: 8 minutes

cooking spray
1 tbsp. butter, melted
¾ pound sea scallops
½ tbsp. fresh thyme, minced
Salt and black pepper, to taste

1. Mix all the ingredients in a medium bowl and toss to coat well.
2. Insert the Drip Tray inside the appliance. Do not insert the Divider.
3. Use the left Control Knob to select Air Fry. Set the cooking temperature to 390°F and the cooking time to 8 minutes. Set the Shake Indicator and press the Start/Pause Button. Let the appliance preheat.
4. When the appliance has preheated, spray XL Crisper Tray with cooking spray and place the scallops on the Crisper Tray. Slide the Crisper Tray into the corresponding shelf position. Flip the scallops halfway through cooking according to the Shake Indicator.
5. When the cooking time has completed, transfer the scallops to a plate. Serve warm.

Classic Fish Sticks

SERVES 4

PREP TIME: 15 minutes
COOK TIME: 15 minutes

Cooking spray
4 fish fillets
2 eggs
1½ cups whole-wheat panko bread crumbs
½ cup whole-wheat flour
1 tsp. seasoned salt
½ tbsp. dried parsley flakes

1. Cut the fish fillets lengthwise into "sticks."
2. In a shallow bowl, combine the whole-wheat flour and seasoned salt.
3. In a small bowl, whisk the eggs with 1 tsp. of water.
4. In another shallow bowl, mix the bread crumbs and parsley flakes.
5. Coat each fish stick in the seasoned flour, then in the egg mixture, and dredge them in the bread crumbs.
6. Insert the Drip Tray inside the appliance. Do not insert the Divider.
7. Use the left Control Knob to select Air Fry. Set the cooking temperature to 400°F and the cooking time to 15 minutes. Set the Shake Indicator and press the Start/Pause Button. Let the appliance preheat.
8. When the appliance has preheated, spray XL Crisper Tray with cooking spray and place the fish sticks in a single layer on the Crisper Tray. Slide the Crisper Tray into the corresponding shelf position. Halfway through cooking, flip the fish sticks according to the Shake Indicator.
9. When the cooking time has completed, transfer the fish sticks to a plate. Serve warm.

Marinated Salmon Fillets

SERVES 4

PREP TIME: 10 minutes
COOK TIME: 15 minutes

Cooking spray
1 tbsp. olive oil
4 (6-ounce / 170-g) salmon fillets, skin-on
¼ cup soy sauce
¼ cup rice wine vinegar
1 tbsp. brown sugar
1 tsp. mustard powder
1 tsp. ground ginger
½ tsp. freshly ground black pepper
½ tsp. minced garlic

1. In a small bowl, combine the olive oil, soy sauce, rice wine vinegar, brown sugar, mustard powder, ginger, black pepper, and garlic to make a marinade.
2. Place the salmon fillets in a shallow baking dish and pour the marinade over them. Cover the baking dish and marinate for at least 1 hour in the refrigerator, turning the fillets occasionally to keep them coated in the marinade.
3. Insert the Drip Tray inside the appliance. Do not insert the Divider.
4. Shake off as much marinade as possible from the fillets and place the fillets in a single layer on the XL Baking Pan, skin-side down. Lightly spray with the cooking spray. Slide the Baking Pan into the corresponding shelf position.
5. Use the left Control Knob to select Roast. Set the cooking temperature to 390°F and the cooking time to 15 minutes. Press the Start/Pause Button to begin the cooking cycle, flipping halfway through cooking.
6. When the cooking time has completed, transfer the fillets to a plate and serve warm.

Grilled Tuna Cakes

PREP TIME: 15 minutes
COOK TIME: 12 minutes

Cooking spray
2 (6-ounces) cans tuna, drained
1 tbsp. fresh lemon juice
1½ tbsps. almond flour
1½ tbsps. mayonnaise
1 tsp. dried dill
1 tsp. garlic powder
½ tsp. onion powder
Pinch of salt and ground black pepper

1. Mix the tuna, almond flour, mayonnaise, lemon juice, dill, and spices in a large bowl.
2. Shape this tuna mixture into 4 equal-sized patties.
3. Insert the Drip Tray inside the appliance. Do not insert the Divider.
4. Spray XL Grill Plate with cooking spray and place the patties. Slide the Grill Plate into the corresponding shelf position.
5. Use the left Control Knob to select Grill. Set the cooking temperature to 390°F and the cooking time to 12 minutes. Press the Start/Pause Button to begin the cooking cycle, flipping halfway through cooking.
6. When the cooking time has completed, transfer the tuna cakes to a plate. Serve warm.

Sesame Glazed Salmon

PREP TIME: 5 minutes
COOK TIME: 15 minutes

Cooking spray
1 tbsp. toasted sesame oil
4 (6-ounce / 170-g) salmon
  fillets, skin-on
3 tbsps. soy sauce

1 tbsp. rice wine or dry sherry
1 tbsp. brown sugar
½ tbsp. sesame seeds
1 tsp. minced garlic
¼ tsp. minced ginger

1. In a small bowl, mix the rice wine, soy sauce, brown sugar, toasted sesame oil, garlic, and ginger.
2. Place the salmon fillets in a shallow baking dish and pour the marinade over the fillets. Cover and refrigerate for at least 1 hour, turning the fillets occasionally to coat in the marinade.
3. Insert the Drip Tray inside the appliance. Do not insert the Divider.
4. Shake off as much marinade as possible and place fillets in a single layer on the XL Grill Plate, skin-side down. Lightly spray with cooking spray. Reserve the marinade. Slide the Grill Plate into the corresponding shelf position.
5. Use the left Control Knob to select Grill. Set the cooking temperature to 390°F and the cooking time to 15 minutes. Press the Start/Pause Button to begin the cooking cycle, flipping halfway through cooking.
6. With 3 minutes remaining, press the Start/Pause Button, brush the tops of the salmon fillets with the reserved marinade and sprinkle with sesame seeds. Press the Start/Pause Button again to continue cooking.
7. When the cooking time has completed, transfer the salmon fillets to a plate. Serve warm.

Cajun-Style Salmon Burgers

SERVES 4

PREP TIME: 10 minutes
COOK TIME: 15 minutes

Cooking spray
4 (5-ounce / 142-g) cans pink salmon in water, any skin and bones
    removed, drained
2 eggs, beaten
1 cup whole-wheat bread crumbs
4 tbsps. light mayonnaise
2 tsps. dry mustard
2 tsps. Cajun seasoning
4 whole-wheat buns

1. In a medium bowl, mix the pink salmon, bread crumbs, eggs, mayonnaise, Cajun seasoning, and dry mustard. Cover with plastic wrap and refrigerate for about 30 minutes.
2. Shape the salmon mixture into four ½-inch-thick patties about the same size as the buns.
3. Insert the Drip Tray inside the appliance. Do not insert the Divider.
4. Place the patties in a single layer on the XL Grill Plate and lightly spray the tops with cooking spray. Slide the Grill Plate into the corresponding shelf position.
5. Use the left Control Knob to select Grill. Set the cooking temperature to 390°F and the cooking time to 15 minutes. Press the Start/Pause Button to begin the cooking cycle.
6. After 8 minutes, press the Start/Pause Button, flip the patties over and lightly spray with cooking spray, and press the Start/Pause Button again to continue cooking.
7. When the cooking time has completed, transfer the patties to a plate. Serve on whole-wheat buns.

Chinese Style Cod

SERVES 2

PREP TIME: 20 minutes
COOK TIME: 15 minutes

3 tbsps. olive oil
2 (7-ounces) cod fillets
1 cup water
¼ cup fresh cilantro, chopped
¼ tsp. sesame oil
2 scallions (green part), sliced
Salt and black pepper, to taste
5 ginger slices
5 little squares rock sugar
5 tbsps. light soy sauce
1 tsp. dark soy sauce

1. Season each cod fillet with salt and black pepper to taste and drizzle with sesame oil.
2. Insert the Drip Tray inside the appliance. Do not insert the Divider.
3. Use the left Control Knob to select Air Fry. Set the cooking temperature to 400°F and the cooking time to 12 minutes. Press the Start/Pause Button. Let the appliance preheat.
4. When the appliance has preheated, spray XL Crisper Tray with cooking spray and place the cod fillets on the Crisper Tray. Slide the Crisper Tray into the corresponding shelf position.
5. Meanwhile, bring water to boil and add the rock sugar and both soy sauces. Cook until sugar is dissolved, continuously stirring and keep aside.
6. When the cooking time has completed, transfer the cod fillets to a plate and top each fillet with cilantro and scallions.
7. Heat the olive oil over medium heat in a small frying pan and add the ginger slices.
8. Sauté for 3 minutes and discard the ginger slices.
9. Drizzle the hot oil over cod fillets and top with the sauce mixture to serve.

Breaded Hake

PREP TIME: 15 minutes COOK TIME: 15 minutes	cooking spray 2 tbsps. vegetable oil 4 (6-ounces) hake fillets	4 ounces breadcrumbs 1 egg 1 lemon, cut into wedges

1. Whisk the egg in a shallow bowl and mix the breadcrumbs and vegetable oil in another bowl.
2. Dip the hake fillets into the whisked egg and then, dredge in the breadcrumb mixture.
3. Insert the Drip Tray inside the appliance. Do not insert the Divider.
4. Use the left Control Knob to select Air Fry. Set the cooking temperature to 390°F and the cooking time to 15 minutes. Set the Shake Indicator and press the Start/Pause Button. Let the appliance preheat.
5. When the appliance has preheated, spray XL Crisper Tray with cooking spray and place the hake fillets in a single layer on the Crisper Tray. Slide the Crisper Tray into the corresponding shelf position. Halfway through cooking, flip the hake fillets over according to the Shake Indicator.
6. When the cooking time has completed, transfer the hake fillets to a plate. Serve with lemon wedges.

Roasted Cod with Broccoli

PREP TIME: 5 minutes COOK TIME: 17 minutes	Cooking spray 2 (6-ounces) fresh cod fillets 1 tbsp. reduced-sodium soy sauce 2 tsps. honey	1 tsp. sesame seeds 4 cups fresh broccoli florets 2 tbsps. butter, melted Salt and black pepper, to taste

1. In a small bowl, combine the soy sauce and honey.
2. Brush the cod fillets with the soy mixture, and top with sesame seeds.
3. Mix the broccoli, butter, salt, and black pepper in a bowl and toss to coat well.
4. Insert the Drip Tray inside the appliance. Insert the Divider.
5. Place the broccoli on the Baking Pan. Slide the Baking Pan into the corresponding shelf position on the left.
6. Use the left Control Knob to select Roast. Set the cooking temperature to 390°F and the cooking time to 17 minutes. Use the right Control Knob to select Air Fry. Set the cooking temperature to 390°F and the cooking time to 15 minutes. Press the Sync Button and the Start/Pause Button to begin the cooking cycle.
7. When the cooking timers of both cooking zones synchronize, press the Start/Pause Button. Spray Crisper Tray with cooking spray and place the cod fillets on the Crisper Tray. Slide the Crisper Tray into the corresponding shelf position on the right. Press the Start/Pause Button again to continue cooking. Flip the cod fillets and shake the broccoli halfway through cooking.
8. When the cooking time has completed, serve fillets with broccoli florets.

Mahi Mahi with Green Beans

PREP TIME: 15 minutes COOK TIME: 15 minutes	1 tbsp. olive oil 4 (6-ounces) Mahi Mahi fillets 5 cups green beans 2 tbsps. fresh dill, chopped	1 tbsp. avocado oil Salt, as required 2 garlic cloves, minced 2 tbsps. fresh lemon juice

1. Combine the dill, garlic, lemon juice, salt and olive oil in a small bowl. Coat Mahi Mahi with this garlic mixture.
2. Mix the green beans, avocado oil and salt in a large bowl.
3. Insert the Drip Tray inside the appliance. Insert the Divider.
4. Place the Mahi Mahi on the Grill Plate. Slide the Grill Plate into the corresponding shelf position on the left. Place the green beans on the Baking Pan. Slide the Baking Pan into the corresponding shelf position on the right.
5. Use the left Control Knob to select Grill. Set the cooking temperature to 400°F and the cooking time to 14 minutes. Use the right Control Knob to select Roast. Set the cooking temperature to 390°F and the cooking time to 15 minutes. Press the Sync Button and the Start/Pause Button to begin the cooking cycle. Flip foods in both zones halfway through cooking.
6. When the cooking time has completed, serve Mahi Mahi immediately with green beans.

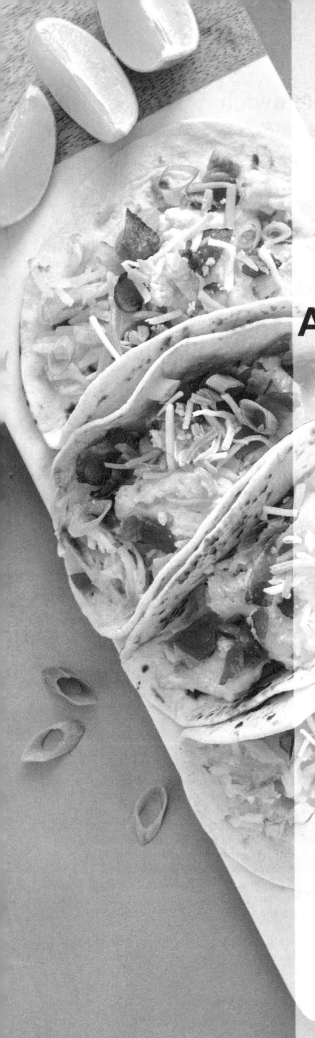

CHAPTER 7
WRAPS, TACOS AND SANDWICHES

Baked Cheese Sandwich

PREP TIME: 5 minutes
COOK TIME: 8 minutes

2 tbsps. mayonnaise
8 slices hot capicola
4 thick slices Brie cheese
4 thick slices sourdough bread

1. Spread the mayonnaise on one side of each slice of bread.
2. Insert the Drip Tray inside the appliance. Do not insert the Divider.
3. Place 2 slices of bread on the XL Grill Plate, mayonnaise-side down. Arrange the slices of Brie and capicola on the bread and cover with the remaining two slices of bread, mayonnaise-side up. Slide the Grill Plate into the corresponding shelf position.
4. Use the left Control Knob to select Grill. Set the cooking temperature to 350°F and the cooking time to 8 minutes. Press the Start/Pause Button to begin the cooking cycle, until the cheese has melted.
5. When the cooking time has completed, serve immediately.

Banana Egg Oatmeal Sandwich

PREP TIME: 5 minutes
COOK TIME: 8 minutes

Cooking spray
1 egg, beaten
8 slices oat nut bread or any whole-grain, oversize bread
2 medium bananas, cut into ½-inch-thick slices
½ cup cornflakes, crushed
¼ cup shredded coconut
6 tbsps. peanut butter
6 tbsps. pineapple preserves

1. In a shallow dish, combine the cornflake crumbs and shredded coconut.
2. For each sandwich, spread one bread slice with 1½ tbsps. of peanut butter. Top with banana slices. Spread another bread slice with 1½ tbsps. of preserves. Combine to make a sandwich.
3. Using a pastry brush, brush top of sandwich lightly with beaten egg. Sprinkle with about 1½ tbsps. of crumb coating, pressing it in to make it stick. Spray with cooking spray.
4. Turn the sandwich over and repeat to coat and spray the other side.
5. Insert the Drip Tray inside the appliance. Do not insert the Divider.
6. Place the sandwiches in a single layer on the XL Grill Plate. Slide the Grill Plate into the corresponding shelf position.
7. Use the left Control Knob to select Grill. Set the cooking temperature to 360°F and the cooking time to 8 minutes. Press the Start/Pause Button to begin the cooking cycle, until coating is golden brown and crispy.
8. When the cooking time has completed, transfer the sandwiches to a plate. Cut the cooked sandwiches in half and serve warm.

Mixed Greens Sandwich

PREP TIME: 15 minutes
COOK TIME: 8 minutes

Cooking spray
2 tsps. olive oil
1½ cups chopped mixed greens
4 slices low-sodium whole-wheat bread
2 slices low-sodium low-fat Swiss cheese
2 garlic cloves, thinly sliced

1. In a skillet over medium heat, add the olive oil, mixed greens and garlic. Cook for 4 to 5 minutes, until the vegetables are tender. Drain, if necessary.
2. Make 2 sandwiches, dividing half of the greens and 1 slice of Swiss cheese between 2 slices of bread. Lightly spray the outsides of the sandwiches with cooking spray.
3. Insert the Drip Tray inside the appliance. Do not insert the Divider.
4. Place the sandwiches on the XL Grill Plate. Slide the Grill Plate into the corresponding shelf position.
5. Use the left Control Knob to select Grill. Set the cooking temperature to 400°F and the cooking time to 8 minutes. Press the Start/Pause Button to begin the cooking cycle, until the bread is toasted and the cheese melts. Flip the sandwiches halfway through cooking.
6. When the cooking time has completed, transfer the sandwiches to a plate. Cut each sandwich in half and serve.

Nugget and Corn Taco Wraps

PREP TIME: 5 minutes
COOK TIME: 18 minutes

cooking spray
1 tbsp. water
4 large corn tortillas
4 pieces commercial vegan nuggets, chopped
2 cups grilled corn kernels
1 small red bell pepper, chopped
1 small yellow onion, diced
Mixed greens, for garnish

1. In a skillet over a medium heat, sauté the nuggets in the water with the onion, corn kernels and bell pepper, then remove from the heat.
2. Fill the tortillas with the nuggets and vegetables and fold them up.
3. Insert the Drip Tray inside the appliance. Do not insert the Divider.
4. Use the left Control Knob to select Air Fry. Set the cooking temperature to 400°F and the cooking time to 18 minutes. Press the Start/Pause Button. Let the appliance preheat.
5. When the appliance has preheated, spray XL Crisper Tray with cooking spray and place the tortillas in a single layer on the Crisper Tray. Slide the Crisper Tray into the corresponding shelf position.
6. When the cooking time has completed, transfer the tortillas to a plate. Serve garnished with the mixed greens.

Cheesy Chicken Sandwich

SERVES 1

PREP TIME: 10 minutes
COOK TIME: 6 minutes

cooking spray
1 tsp. olive oil
1 hamburger bun
⅓ cup chicken, cooked and shredded
¼ cup shredded cabbage
2 Mozzarella slices
2 tsps. butter, melted

1 tsp. mayonnaise
½ tsp. balsamic vinegar
¼ tsp. smoked paprika
¼ tsp. black pepper
¼ tsp. garlic powder
Pinch of salt

1. Brush some butter onto the outside of the hamburger bun.
2. In a small bowl, coat the shredded chicken with the garlic powder, salt, pepper, and paprika.
3. In a separate bowl, stir together the mayonnaise, olive oil, cabbage, and balsamic vinegar to make coleslaw.
4. Slice the bun in two. Start building the sandwich, starting with the chicken, followed by the Mozzarella, the coleslaw, and finally the top bun.
5. Insert the Drip Tray inside the appliance. Do not insert the Divider.
6. Spray XL Crisper Tray with cooking spray. Place the sandwich on the Crisper Tray and slide the Crisper Tray into the corresponding shelf position.
7. Use the left Control Knob to select Bake. Set the cooking temperature to 370°F and the cooking time to 6 minutes. Press the Start/Pause Button to begin the cooking cycle.
8. When the cooking time has completed, serve immediately.

Cheesy Shrimp Sandwich

SERVES 4

PREP TIME: 10 minutes
COOK TIME: 7 minutes

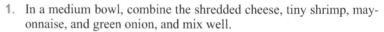

1 (6-ounce / 170-g) can tiny shrimp, drained
1¼ cups shredded Colby, Cheddar, or Havarti cheese
4 slices whole grain or whole-wheat bread
3 tbsps. mayonnaise
2 tbsps. minced green onion
2 tbsps. softened butter

1. In a medium bowl, combine the shredded cheese, tiny shrimp, mayonnaise, and green onion, and mix well.
2. Spread this mixture on two of the slices of bread. Top with the other slices of bread to make two sandwiches. Spread the sandwiches lightly with butter.
3. Insert the Drip Tray inside the appliance. Do not insert the Divider.
4. Place the sandwiches on the XL Grill Plate. Slide the Grill Plate into the corresponding shelf position.
5. Use the left Control Knob to select Grill. Set the cooking temperature to 400°F and the cooking time to 7 minutes. Press the Start/Pause Button to begin the cooking cycle, until the bread is browned and crisp and the cheese is melted.
6. When the cooking time has completed, cut in half and serve warm.

Tuna and Lettuce Wraps

SERVES 4

PREP TIME: 10 minutes
COOK TIME: 7 minutes

cooking spray
1 pound (454 g) fresh tuna steak
4 low-sodium whole-wheat tortillas
2 cups shredded romaine lettuce
1 red bell pepper, thinly sliced
¼ cup low-fat mayonnaise
1 tbsp. grated fresh ginger
2 garlic cloves, minced
½ tsp. toasted sesame oil

1. In a medium bowl, mix the tuna cubes, ginger, garlic, and sesame oil. Let it stand for 10 minutes.
2. Insert the Drip Tray inside the appliance. Do not insert the Divider.
3. Use the left Control Knob to select Air Fry. Set the cooking temperature to 390°F and the cooking time to 7 minutes. Set the Shake Indicator and press the Start/Pause Button. Let the appliance preheat.
4. When the appliance has preheated, spray XL Crisper Tray with cooking spray and place the tuna on the Crisper Tray. Slide the Crisper Tray into the corresponding shelf position. Shake tuna halfway through cooking according to the Shake Indicator.
5. When the cooking time has completed, transfer the tuna to a plate. Make the wraps with the tuna, tortillas, mayonnaise, lettuce and bell pepper. Serve immediately.

Vegetable and White Fish Tacos

SERVES 4

PREP TIME: 10 minutes
COOK TIME: 9 minutes

2 tsps. olive oil
1 pound (454 g) white fish fillets
3 tbsps. freshly squeezed lemon juice, divided
1½ cups chopped red cabbage
1 large carrot, grated
½ cup low-sodium salsa
⅓ cup low-fat Greek yogurt
4 soft low-sodium whole-wheat tortillas

1. Brush the white fish fillets with the olive oil and sprinkle with 1 tbsp. of lemon juice.
2. Insert the Drip Tray inside the appliance. Do not insert the Divider.
3. Place the fish fillets on the XL Baking Pan. Slide the Baking Pan into the corresponding shelf position.
4. Use the left Control Knob to select Roast. Set the cooking temperature to 400°F and the cooking time to 9 minutes. Press the Start/Pause Button to begin the cooking cycle, until the fish just flakes when tested with a fork.
5. Meanwhile, stir together the remaining 2 tbsps. of lemon juice, the red cabbage, carrot, salsa, and yogurt in a medium bowl.
6. When the cooking time has completed, transfer the fish to a plate and break it up into large pieces.
7. Offer the fish, tortillas, and the cabbage mixture, and let each person assemble a taco.
8. Serve warm.

Fajita Meatball Lettuce Wraps

SERVES 4

PREP TIME: 10 minutes COOK TIME: 14 minutes	Cooking spray 1 pound (454 g) 85% lean ground beef ½ cup salsa, plus more for serving ¼ cup diced green or red bell peppers ¼ cup chopped onions 1 large egg, beaten 1 clove garlic, minced	1 tsp. fine sea salt ½ tsp. ground cumin ½ tsp. chili powder For Serving: Pico de gallo or salsa 8 leaves Boston lettuce Lime slices

1. In a large bowl, mix together all the ingredients until well combined.
2. Shape the beef mixture into eight 1-inch balls.
3. Insert the Drip Tray inside the appliance. Do not insert the Divider.
4. Spray XL Baking Pan with cooking spray and place the balls in a single layer. Slide the Baking Pan into the corresponding shelf position.
5. Use the left Control Knob to select Roast. Set the cooking temperature to 350°F and the cooking time to 14 minutes. Press the Start/Pause Button to begin the cooking cycle, shaking halfway through cooking.
6. When the cooking time has completed, serve each meatball on a lettuce leaf, topped with pico de gallo or salsa. Serve with lime slices.

Turkey, Hummus, and Cheese Wraps

SERVES 4

PREP TIME: 10 minutes COOK TIME: 8 minutes	cooking spray 4 large whole wheat wraps 16 thin slices deli turkey	8 slices provolone cheese 1 cup fresh baby spinach, or more to taste ½ cup hummus

1. To assemble, place 2 tbsps. of hummus on each wrap and spread to within about a half inch from edges. Top with 4 slices of turkey and 2 slices of provolone. Finish with ¼ cup of baby spinach, or pile on as much as you like.
2. Roll up each wrap. You don't need to fold or seal the ends.
3. Insert the Drip Tray inside the appliance. Do not insert the Divider.
4. Use the left Control Knob to select Air Fry. Set the cooking temperature to 360°F and the cooking time to 8 minutes. Press the Start/Pause Button. Let the appliance preheat.
5. When the appliance has preheated, spray XL Crisper Tray with cooking spray and place the wraps on the Crisper Tray, seam-side down. Slide the Crisper Tray into the corresponding shelf position.
6. When the cooking time has completed, transfer the wraps to a plate. Serve warm.

Bacon and Bell Pepper Sandwich

SERVES 4

PREP TIME: 10 minutes COOK TIME: 12 minutes	2 tbsps. honey 3 pita pockets, cut in half 8 slices cooked bacon, cut into thirds 1¼ cups torn butter lettuce leaves	2 tomatoes, sliced 1 red bell pepper, sliced 1 yellow bell pepper, sliced ⅓ cup spicy barbecue sauce

1. In a small bowl, combine the spicy barbecue sauce and honey. Brush this mixture lightly onto the bacon slices and the red and yellow pepper slices.
2. Place the peppers on the Baking Pan. Slide the Baking Pan into the corresponding shelf position on the left.
3. Use the left Control Knob to select Roast. Set the cooking temperature to 390°F and the cooking time to 12 minutes. Use the right Control Knob to select Air Fry. Set the cooking temperature to 350°F and the cooking time to 6 minutes. Press the Sync Button and the Start/Pause Button to begin the cooking cycle.
4. When the cooking timers of both cooking zones synchronize, press the Start/Pause Button. Place the bacon on the Crisper Tray and slide the Crisper Tray into the corresponding shelf position on the right. Press the Start/Pause Button again to continue cooking. Shake foods in both zones halfway through cooking.
5. When the cooking time has completed, fill the pita halves with the bacon, peppers, any remaining barbecue sauce, lettuce, and tomatoes, and enjoy.

CHAPTER 8
LAMB

Fantastic Leg of Lamb

SERVES 4

PREP TIME: 10 minutes
COOK TIME: 50 minutes

2 tbsps. olive oil
2 pounds leg of lamb
2 fresh thyme sprigs
2 fresh rosemary sprigs
Salt and black pepper, to taste

1. Coat the leg of lamb with oil, salt and black pepper and wrap with herb sprigs.
2. Insert the Drip Tray inside the appliance. Do not insert the Divider.
3. Slide the leg of lamb onto the Rotisserie Shaft and secure the lamb with the Rotisserie Forks. Secure the Rotisserie Shaft in the appliance.
4. Use the left Control Knob to select Rotisserie. Set the cooking temperature to 400°F and the cooking time to 50 minutes. Press the Start/Pause Button to begin the cooking cycle.
5. After 40 minutes, start checking the internal temperature with an instant-read thermometer inserted into the thickest part of the lamb. Cook until the desired doneness is reached.
6. When the cooking time has completed, transfer the leg of lamb to a plate. Serve warm.

Lamb with Potatoes

SERVES 2

PREP TIME: 20 minutes
COOK TIME: 30 minutes

½ pound lamb meat
2 small potatoes, peeled and halved
½ small onion, peeled and halved
1 garlic clove, crushed
½ tbsp. dried rosemary, crushed
1 tsp. olive oil

1. Rub the lamb meat evenly with garlic and rosemary.
2. Add the potatoes in a large bowl and stir in the olive oil and onions.
3. Insert the Drip Tray inside the appliance. Insert the Divider.
4. Place the vegetables on the Baking Pan. Slide the Baking Pan into the corresponding shelf position on the left. Place the lamb meat on the Grill Plate. Slide the Grill Plate into the corresponding shelf position on the right.
5. Use the left Control Knob to select Roast. Set the cooking temperature to 400°F and the cooking time to 30 minutes. Use the right Control Knob to select Grill. Set the cooking temperature to 390°F and the cooking time to 25 minutes. Press the Sync Button and the Start/Pause Button to begin the cooking cycle. Flip the foods in both zones halfway through cooking.
6. When the cooking time has completed, serve lamb with vegetables.

Za'atar Lamb Loin Chops

PREP TIME: 10 minutes
COOK TIME: 16 minutes

1 tsp. olive oil
8 (3½-ounces) bone-in lamb loin chops, trimmed
3 garlic cloves, crushed
1 tbsp. Za'atar
1 tbsp. fresh lemon juice
Salt and black pepper, to taste

1. Mix the garlic, lemon juice, oil, Za'atar, salt, and black pepper in a large bowl.
2. Coat the lamb chops generously with the herb mixture.
3. Insert the Drip Tray inside the appliance. Do not insert the Divider.
4. Place the chops in a single layers on the XL Baking Pan. Slide the Baking Pan into the corresponding shelf position.
5. Use the left Control Knob to select Roast. Set the cooking temperature to 400°F and the cooking time to 16 minutes. Press the Start/Pause Button to begin the cooking cycle, flipping halfway through cooking.
6. When the cooking time has completed, transfer the chops to a plate and serve warm.

(Note: Za'atar - Za'atar is generally made with ground dried thyme, oregano, marjoram, or some combination thereof, mixed with toasted sesame seeds, and salt, though other spices such as sumac might also be added. Some commercial varieties also include roasted flour.)

Classic Lamb Satay

PREP TIME: 5 minutes
COOK TIME: 10 minutes

Cooking spray
2 boneless lamb steaks
1 tsp. ginger
¼ tsp. cumin
½ tsp. nutmeg
Salt and ground black pepper, to taste

1. Combine the cumin, ginger, nutmeg, salt and pepper in a medium bowl.
2. Cube the lamb steaks and massage the spice mixture into each one.
3. Let marinate for about 10 minutes, then transfer onto metal skewers.
4. Insert the Drip Tray inside the appliance. Do not insert the Divider.
5. Use the left Control Knob to select Air Fry. Set the cooking temperature to 400°F and the cooking time to 10 minutes. Set the Shake Indicator and press the Start/Pause Button. Let the appliance preheat.
6. When the appliance has preheated, spray XL Crisper Tray with cooking spray and place the skewers on the Crisper Tray. Slide the Crisper Tray into the corresponding shelf position. Halfway through cooking, flip the skewers over according to the Shake Indicator.
7. When the cooking time has completed, transfer the skewers to a plate. Serve warm.

Garlicky Lamb Chops

SERVES 2

PREP TIME: 20 minutes
COOK TIME: 17 minutes

¼ cup olive oil, divided
1 tbsp. fresh oregano, chopped
1 tbsp. fresh thyme, chopped
8 (4-ounce) lamb chops
1 bulb garlic, halved
Salt and black pepper, to taste

1. Rub the garlic bulb halves with about 2 tbsps. of the olive oil.
2. Mix the remaining olive oil, herbs, salt and black pepper in a large bowl. Coat the lamb chops with about 1 tbsp. of the herb mixture.
3. Insert the Drip Tray inside the appliance. Do not insert the Divider.
4. Place the lamb chops and garlic bulb halves on the XL Grill Plate. Slide the Grill Plate into the corresponding shelf position.
5. Use the left Control Knob to select Grill. Set the cooking temperature to 390°F and the cooking time to 17 minutes. Press the Start/Pause Button to begin the cooking cycle, flipping the lamb chops halfway through cooking.
6. When the cooking time has completed, transfer the lamb chops to a plate and serve with herb mixture.

Spiced Lamb Steaks

SERVES 3

PREP TIME: 15 minutes
COOK TIME: 15 minutes

1½ pounds boneless lamb sirloin steaks
½ onion, roughly chopped
5 garlic cloves, peeled
1 tbsp. fresh ginger, peeled
1 tsp. garam masala
1 tsp. ground fennel
½ tsp. ground cinnamon
½ tsp. ground cumin
½ tsp. cayenne pepper
Salt and black pepper, to taste

1. Put the onion, ginger, garlic and spices in a blender and pulse until smooth.
2. Coat the lamb steaks with this mixture on both sides and refrigerate to marinate for about 24 hours.
3. Insert the Drip Tray inside the appliance. Do not insert the Divider.
4. Place the lamb steaks on the XL Grill Plate. Slide the Grill Plate into the corresponding shelf position.
5. Use the left Control Knob to select Grill. Set the cooking temperature to 390°F and the cooking time to 15 minutes. Press the Start/Pause Button to begin the cooking cycle, flipping halfway through cooking.
6. When the cooking time has completed, transfer the lamb steaks to a plate and serve warm.

Air Fried Lamb Ribs Mint Yogurt

SERVES 4

PREP TIME: 5 minutes COOK TIME: 18 minutes	cooking spray 1 pound (454 g) lamb ribs 2 tbsps. mustard 1 tsp. rosemary, chopped Salt and ground black pepper, to taste 1 cup Green yogurt ¼ cup mint leaves, chopped

1. Apply the mustard to the lamb ribs with a brush, and season with rosemary, salt, and pepper.
2. Insert the Drip Tray inside the appliance. Do not insert the Divider.
3. Use the left Control Knob to select Air Fry. Set the cooking temperature to 390°F and the cooking time to 18 minutes. Set the Shake Indicator and press the Start/Pause Button. Let the appliance preheat.
4. When the appliance has preheated, spray XL Crisper Tray with cooking spray and place the lamb ribs on the Crisper Tray. Slide the Crisper Tray into the corresponding shelf position. Halfway through cooking, flip the lamb ribs over according to the Shake Indicator.
5. Meanwhile, combine the mint leaves and yogurt in a small bowl.
6. When the cooking time has completed, transfer the lamb ribs to a plate and serve with the mint yogurt.

Italian Lamb Chops with Avocado Mayo

SERVES 2

PREP TIME: 5 minutes COOK TIME: 12 minutes	2 lamb chops 2 avocados ½ cup mayonnaise 1 tbsp. lemon juice 2 tsps. Italian herbs

1. Season the lamb chops with the Italian herbs, then set aside for about 5 minutes.
2. Insert the Drip Tray inside the appliance. Do not insert the Divider.
3. Place the lamb chops on the XL Grill Plate. Slide the Grill Plate into the corresponding shelf position.
4. Use the left Control Knob to select Grill. Set the cooking temperature to 400°F and the cooking time to 12 minutes. Press the Start/Pause Button to begin the cooking cycle, flipping halfway through cooking.
5. Meanwhile, halve the avocados and open to remove the pits. Spoon the flesh into a blender. Add the mayonnaise and lemon juice and pulse until a smooth consistency is achieved.
6. When the cooking time has completed, transfer the lamb chops to a plate. Serve warm with the avocado mayo.

Mustard Lamb Loin Chops

SERVES 4

PREP TIME: 15 minutes COOK TIME: 18 minutes	½ tsp. olive oil 8 (4-ounces) lamb loin chops 1 tbsp. fresh lemon juice 2 tbsps. Dijon mustard 1 tsp. dried tarragon Salt and black pepper, to taste

1. Mix the mustard, lemon juice, olive oil, tarragon, salt, and black pepper in a large bowl.
2. Coat the lamb chops generously with this mustard mixture.
3. Insert the Drip Tray inside the appliance. Do not insert the Divider.
4. Place the chops in a single layer on the XL Baking Pan. Slide the Baking Pan into the corresponding shelf position.
5. Use the left Control Knob to select Roast. Set the cooking temperature to 390°F and the cooking time to 18 minutes. Press the Start/Pause Button to begin the cooking cycle, flipping halfway through cooking.
6. When the cooking time has completed, transfer the chops to a plate. Serve hot.

Herbed Lamb Burger

PREP TIME: 15 minutes COOK TIME: 22-23 minutes	2 tsps. olive oil 1 pound (454 g) ground lamb ⅓ onion, finely chopped ½ cup black olives, finely chopped ⅓ cup crumbled feta cheese 1 clove garlic, minced 2 tbsps. fresh parsley, finely chopped 1½ tsps. fresh oregano, finely chopped ½ tsp. salt freshly ground black pepper 4 thick pita breads toppings and condiments

1. In a medium skillet over medium-high heat, add the olive oil and cook the onion until tender, but not browned about 4 to 5 minutes. Place the garlic and cook for another minute. Transfer the onion and garlic to a mixing bowl and add the ground lamb, parsley, oregano, olives, feta cheese, salt and pepper. Gently mix the ingredients together.
2. Divide the lamb mixture into 4 equal portions and then form the hamburgers, being careful not to over-handle the meat. One good way to do this is to throw the meat back and forth between the hands like a baseball, packing the meat each time you catch it. Flatten the balls into patties, making an indentation in the center of each patty. Flatten the sides of the patties as well.
3. Insert the Drip Tray inside the appliance. Do not insert the Divider.
4. Place the burgers in a single layer on the XL Grill Plate. Slide the Grill Plate into the corresponding shelf position.
5. Use the left Control Knob to select Grill. Set the cooking temperature to 370°F and the cooking time to 16 minutes. Press the Start/Pause Button to begin the cooking cycle, flipping halfway through cooking.
6. When the cooking time has completed, transfer the burgers to a plate and let the burgers rest for a few minutes before dressing and serving.
7. While the burgers are resting, bake the pita breads in the airfryer for 2 minutes. Tuck the burgers into the toasted pita breads, or wrap the pitas around the burgers and serve with a tzatziki sauce or some mayonnaise.

Nut Crusted Rack of Lamb

PREP TIME: 15 minutes COOK TIME: 35 minutes	1 tbsp. olive oil 1¾ pounds rack of lamb 1 egg 3-ounce almonds, chopped finely 1 tbsp. breadcrumbs 1 tbsp. fresh rosemary, chopped 1 garlic clove, minced Salt and black pepper, to taste

1. Mix the olive oil, garlic, salt and black pepper in a bowl.
2. Whisk the egg in a shallow dish and mix breadcrumbs, almonds and rosemary in another shallow dish.
3. Coat the rack of lamb with the garlic mixture evenly, dip into the egg and dredge into the breadcrumb mixture.
4. Insert the Drip Tray inside the appliance. Do not insert the Divider.
5. Place the rack of lamb on the XL Baking Pan. Slide the Baking Pan into the corresponding shelf position.
6. Use the left Control Knob to select Roast. Set the cooking temperature to 390°F and the cooking time to 35 minutes. Press the Start/Pause Button to begin the cooking cycle, flipping halfway through cooking.
7. When the cooking time has completed, transfer the rack of lamb to a plate. Serve warm.

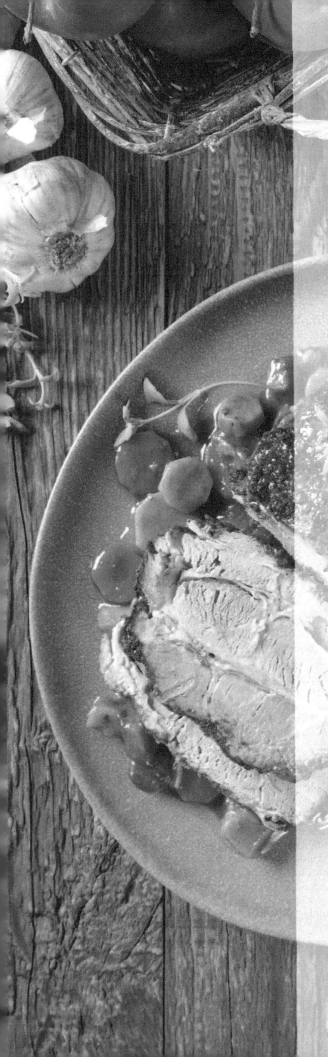

CHAPTER 9
PORK

Marinated Pork

SERVES 4 TO 6

PREP TIME: 10 minutes
COOK TIME: 35 minutes

¼ cup olive oil
2 pounds (907 g) pork tenderloin
¼ cup freshly squeezed lemon juice
¼ cup soy sauce

1 garlic clove, minced
1 tbsp. Dijon mustard
1 tsp. salt
½ tsp. freshly ground black pepper

1. In a large mixing bowl, make the marinade: Mix the olive oil, lemon juice, soy sauce, minced garlic, Dijon mustard, salt, and pepper. Reserve ¼ cup of the marinade.
2. Place the pork tenderloin in a large bowl and pour the remaining marinade over the meat. Cover and marinate in the refrigerator for about 1 hour.
3. Insert the Drip Tray inside the appliance. Do not insert the Divider.
4. Slide the marinated pork tenderloin onto the Rotisserie Shaft and secure the pork tenderloin with the Rotisserie Forks. Secure the Rotisserie Shaft in the appliance.
5. Use the left Control Knob to select Rotisserie. Set the cooking temperature to 375°F and the cooking time to 35 minutes. Press the Start/Pause Button to begin the cooking cycle, brushing with the reserved marinade twice in between.
6. After 30 minutes, start checking the internal temperature with an instant-read thermometer inserted into the thickest part of the pork. Cook until the desired doneness is reached.
7. When the cooking time has completed, let sit for 8 minutes to rest before slicing.

Pork Loin with Potatoes

SERVES 5

PREP TIME: 15 minutes
COOK TIME: 35 minutes

cooking spray
3 tbsps. olive oil, divided
2 pounds pork loin
3 large red potatoes, chopped

1 tsp. fresh parsley, chopped
½ tsp. garlic powder
½ tsp. red pepper flakes, crushed
Salt and ground black pepper, as required

1. Rub the pork loin evenly with 1½ tbsps. olive oil, parsley, salt, and black pepper.
2. Mix the red potatoes, remaining oil, garlic powder, red pepper flakes, salt, and black pepper in a medium bowl.
3. Insert the Drip Tray inside the appliance. Insert the Divider.
4. Place the pork loin on the Baking Pan. Slide the Baking Pan into the corresponding shelf position on the left.
5. Use the left Control Knob to select Roast. Set the cooking temperature to 375°F and the cooking time to 35 minutes. Use the right Control Knob to select Air Fry. Set the cooking temperature to 400°F and the cooking time to 30 minutes. Press the Sync Button and the Start/Pause Button to begin the cooking cycle.
6. When the cooking timers of both cooking zones synchronize, press the Start/Pause Button. Spray Crisper Tray with cooking spray and place the potatoes on the Crisper Tray. Slide the Crisper Tray into the corresponding shelf position on the right. Press the Start/Pause Button again to continue cooking. Halfway through cooking, flip the pork loin over and shake the potatoes.
7. When the cooking time has completed, transfer the pork loin and potatoes to a bowl. Cut pork loin into desired size slices and serve alongside potatoes.

Barbecue Pork Ribs with Green Beans

SERVES 4

PREP TIME: 5 minutes
COOK TIME: 30 minutes

1 pound (454 g) pork ribs, chopped
1 pound green beans, trimmed and
  halved
1 tbsp. barbecue dry rub
1 tsp. mustard

1 tbsp. apple cider vinegar
1 tsp. sesame oil
1 tsp. unsalted butter, melted
¼ tsp. garlic powder

1. Combine the dry rub, mustard, apple cider vinegar, and sesame oil in a small bowl, then coat the ribs with this mixture. Refrigerate the ribs for 20 minutes.
2. Mix the green beans, butter and garlic powder in a medium bowl and toss to coat well.
3. Insert the Drip Tray inside the appliance. Insert the Divider.
4. Place the ribs on the Grill Plate. Slide the Grill Plate into the corresponding shelf position on the left. Place the green beans on the Baking Pan. Slide the Baking Pan into the corresponding shelf position on the right.
5. Use the left Control Knob to select Grill. Set the cooking temperature to 390°F and the cooking time to 30 minutes. Use the right Control Knob to select Roast. Set the cooking temperature to 390°F and the cooking time to 15 minutes. Press the Sync Button and the Start/Pause Button to begin the cooking cycle. Halfway through cooking, flip the ribs and green beans over.
6. When the cooking time has completed, serve ribs with green beans.

Mexican Pork Chops

SERVES 2

PREP TIME: 5 minutes
COOK TIME: 14 minutes

2 tbsps. unsalted butter, divided
2 (4-ounce / 113-g) boneless pork chops
1½ tsps. taco seasoning mix
¼ tsp. dried oregano

1. Combine the dried oregano and taco seasoning in a small bowl and rub the mixture into the pork chops. Brush the pork chops with 1 tbsp. butter.
2. Insert the Drip Tray inside the appliance. Do not insert the Divider.
3. Place the pork chops on the XL Grill Plate. Slide the Grill Plate into the corresponding shelf position.
4. Use the left Control Knob to select Grill. Set the cooking temperature to 390°F and the cooking time to 14 minutes. Press the Start/Pause Button to begin the cooking cycle, flipping halfway through cooking.
5. When the cooking time has completed, transfer the pork chops to a plate. Serve with a garnish of remaining butter.

Homemade Sausage Meatballs

PREP TIME: 15 minutes
COOK TIME: 14 minutes

cooking spray
3½-ounce sausage, casing removed
½ medium onion, minced finely
1 tsp. fresh sage, chopped finely
3 tbsps. Italian breadcrumbs
½ tsp. garlic, minced
Salt and black pepper, to taste

1. Mix all the ingredients in a medium bowl until well combined.
2. Shape the sausage mixture into equal-sized balls.
3. Insert the Drip Tray inside the appliance. Do not insert the Divider.
4. Use the left Control Knob to select Air Fry. Set the cooking temperature to 390°F and the cooking time to 14 minutes. Set the Shake Indicator and press the Start/Pause Button. Let the appliance preheat.
5. When the appliance has preheated, spray XL Crisper Tray with cooking spray and place the balls on the Crisper Tray. Slide the Crisper Tray into the corresponding shelf position. Shake balls halfway through cooking according to the Shake Indicator.
6. When the cooking time has completed, transfer the balls to a plate and serve warm.

Air Fried Baby Back Ribs

SERVES 2

PREP TIME: 5 minutes
COOK TIME: 30 minutes

2 baby back ribs
3 cloves minced garlic
2 tsps. red pepper flakes
¾ tsp. ground ginger
Salt and ground black pepper, to taste

1. Mix the red pepper flakes, ginger, garlic, salt and pepper in a small bowl, making sure to combine well. Massage the mixture into the baby back ribs.
2. Insert the Drip Tray inside the appliance. Do not insert the Divider.
3. Use the left Control Knob to select Air Fry. Set the cooking temperature to 375°F and the cooking time to 30 minutes. Set the Shake Indicator and press the Start/Pause Button. Let the appliance preheat.
4. When the appliance has preheated, spray XL Crisper Tray with cooking spray and place the baby back ribs on the Crisper Tray. Slide the Crisper Tray into the corresponding shelf position. Halfway through cooking, flip the baby back ribs over according to the Shake Indicator.
5. When the cooking time has completed, transfer the baby back ribs to a plate. Serve warm.

Citrus Pork Loin Roast

SERVES 8

PREP TIME: 10 minutes
COOK TIME: 40 minutes

2 pound (907 g) boneless pork loin roast
2 tbsps. olive oil
1 tbsp. lime juice
1 tbsp. orange marmalade
1 tsp. coarse brown mustard
1 tsp. curry powder
1 tsp. dried lemongrass
Salt and ground black pepper, to taste

1. Mix the olive oil, lime juice, marmalade, mustard, curry powder and lemongrass in a small bowl.
2. Rub this mixture all over the surface of the pork loin. Season with salt and pepper.
3. Insert the Drip Tray inside the appliance. Do not insert the Divider.
4. Slide the pork roast onto the Rotisserie Shaft and secure the pork roast with the Rotisserie Forks. Secure the Rotisserie Shaft in the appliance.
5. Use the left Control Knob to select Rotisserie. Set the cooking temperature to 375°F and the cooking time to 40 minutes. Press the Start/Pause Button to begin the cooking cycle.
6. After 35 minutes, start checking the internal temperature with an instant-read thermometer inserted into the thickest part of the pork. Cook until the desired doneness is reached.
7. When the cooking time has completed, wrap roast in foil and let rest for 10 minutes before slicing.

Cheese Crusted Chops

SERVES 6

PREP TIME: 10 minutes
COOK TIME: 18 minutes

Cooking spray
6 thick boneless pork chops
1 cup pork rind crumbs
2 beaten eggs
3 tbsps. grated Parmesan cheese
¼ tsp. chili powder
½ tsp. onion powder
½ tsp. salt
¼ tsp. pepper
1 tsp. smoked paprika

1. Rub the salt and pepper on both sides of pork chops.
2. In a food processor, pulse the pork rinds into crumbs. Mix the crumbs with chili powder, onion powder, and paprika in a bowl.
3. Beat the eggs in another bowl.
4. Dip the pork chops into eggs then into pork rind crumb mixture.
5. Insert the Drip Tray inside the appliance. Do not insert the Divider.
6. Use the left Control Knob to select Air Fry. Set the cooking temperature to 390°F and the cooking time to 18 minutes. Set the Shake Indicator and press the Start/Pause Button. Let the appliance preheat.
7. When the appliance has preheated, spray XL Crisper Tray with cooking spray and place the pork chops in a single layer on the Crisper Tray. Slide the Crisper Tray into the corresponding shelf position. Halfway through cooking, flip the pork chops over according to the Shake Indicator.
8. When the cooking time has completed, transfer the pork chops to a plate. Serve garnished with the Parmesan cheese.

Pork and Enoki Mushroom Rolls

SERVES 6

PREP TIME: 10 minutes COOK TIME: 17 minutes	cooking spray 6 (4-ounce / 113-g) pork belly slices 6 ounces (170 g) Enoki mushrooms 4 tbsps. brown sugar	4 tbsps. mirin 4 tbsps. soy sauce 2-inch ginger, chopped 1 tsp. almond flour

1. Mix the brown sugar, mirin, soy sauce, almond flour, and ginger together until brown sugar dissolves.
2. Take pork belly slices and wrap around a bundle of mushrooms. Brush each roll with teriyaki sauce. Chill for half an hour.
3. Insert the Drip Tray inside the appliance. Do not insert the Divider.
4. Use the left Control Knob to select Air Fry. Set the cooking temperature to 390°F and the cooking time to 17 minutes. Set the Shake Indicator and press the Start/Pause Button. Let the appliance preheat.
5. When the appliance has preheated, spray XL Crisper Tray with cooking spray and place the rolls in a single layer on the Crisper Tray. Slide the Crisper Tray into the corresponding shelf position. Halfway through cooking, flip the rolls over according to the Shake Indicator.
6. When the cooking time has completed, transfer the rolls to a plate. Serve warm.

Pork Burgers

SERVES 8

PREP TIME: 15 minutes COOK TIME: 15 minutes	21-ounce ground pork 2 small onions, chopped 8 burger buns ½ cup cheddar cheese, grated 2 tsps. mustard 2 tsps. dried mixed herbs, crushed	2 tsps. fresh basil, chopped 2 tsps. garlic puree 2 tsps. tomato puree Salt and freshly ground black pepper, to taste

1. Mix all the ingredients in a large bowl except the cheese and buns.
2. Shape this pork mixture into 8 equal-sized patties.
3. Insert the Drip Tray inside the appliance. Do not insert the Divider.
4. Place the patties in a single layer on the XL Grill Plate. Slide the Grill Plate into the corresponding shelf position.
5. Use the left Control Knob to select Grill. Set the cooking temperature to 390°F and the cooking time to 15 minutes. Press the Start/Pause Button to begin the cooking cycle, flipping halfway through cooking.
6. When the cooking time has completed, arrange the patties in buns with cheese to serve.

Whiskey Glazed Ham

SERVES 4

PREP TIME: 10 minutes COOK TIME: 35 minutes	¾ cup whiskey 1 (1 pound) ham joint 2 tbsps. honey 2 tbsps. French mustard

1. Mix all the ingredients in a bowl except the ham.
2. Keep the ham joint for about 30 minutes at room temperature.
3. Insert the Drip Tray inside the appliance. Do not insert the Divider.
4. Place the ham joint on the XL Baking Pan and top with half of the whiskey mixture. Slide the Baking Pan into the corresponding shelf position.
5. Use the left Control Knob to select Roast. Set the cooking temperature to 390°F and the cooking time to 35 minutes. Press the Start/Pause Button to begin the cooking cycle.
6. After 20 minutes, press the Start/Pause Button, flip the ham joint over and coat with the remaining whiskey mixture, and press the Start/Pause Button again to continue cooking.
7. When the cooking time has completed, transfer the ham joint to a plate. Serve warm.

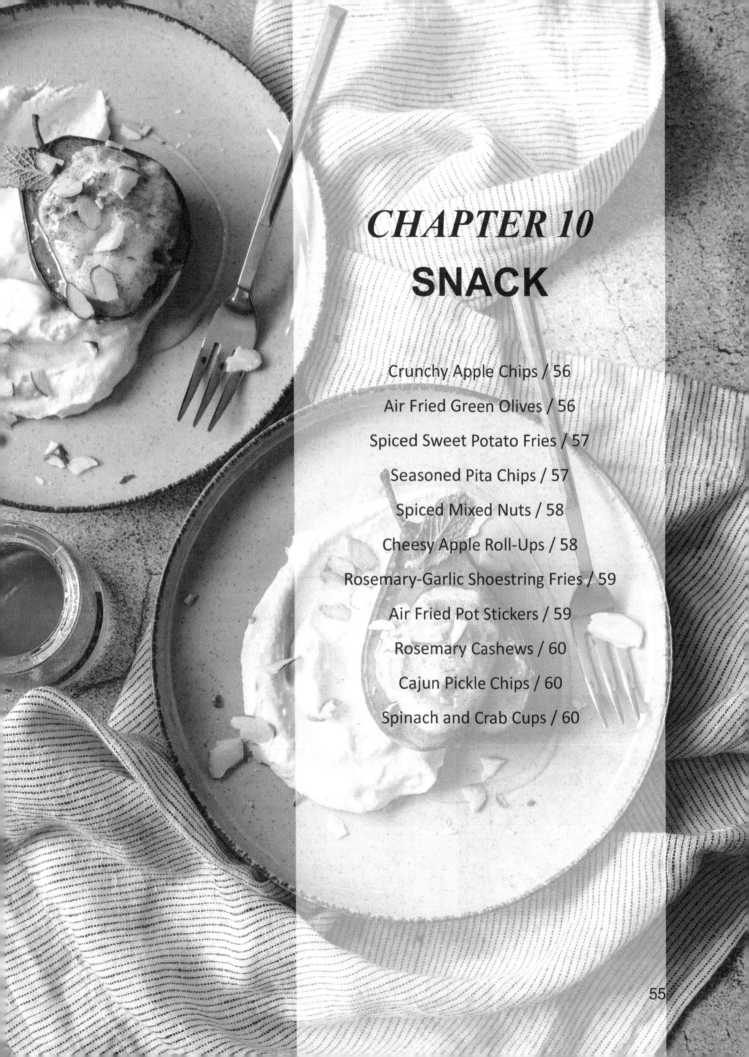

CHAPTER 10
SNACK

Crunchy Apple Chips

SERVES 2

PREP TIME: 5 minutes
COOK TIME: 8 hours

2 Honeycrisp or Pink Lady apples

1. Core the apples with an apple corer, leaving apple whole. Cut the apples into ⅛-inch-thick slices.
2. Insert the Drip Tray inside the appliance. Do not insert the Divider.
3. Place the apple slices in a single layer on the XL Crisper Tray. Slide the Crisper Tray into the corresponding shelf position.
4. Use the left Control Knob to select Dehydrate. Set the cooking temperature to 135°F and the cooking time to 5 hours. Press the Start/Pause Button to begin the cooking cycle.
5. When the cooking time has completed, place the apple chips in a single layer on a wire rack to cool. Apples will become crisper as they cool. Serve immediately.

Air Fried Green Olives

SERVES 4

PREP TIME: 5 minutes
COOK TIME: 8 minutes

Cooking spray
1 (5½-ounce / 156-g) jar pitted green olives
1 egg
½ cup all-purpose flour
½ cup bread crumbs
Salt and pepper, to taste

1. Remove the green olives from the jar and dry thoroughly with paper towels.
2. In a small bowl, combine the flour with salt and pepper. Place the bread crumbs in another small bowl. In a third small bowl, beat the egg.
3. Dip the olives in the flour, then the egg, and then the bread crumbs.
4. Insert the Drip Tray inside the appliance. Do not insert the Divider.
5. Use the left Control Knob to select Air Fry. Set the cooking temperature to 400°F and the cooking time to 8 minutes. Set the Shake Indicator and press the Start/Pause Button. Let the appliance preheat.
6. When the appliance has preheated, spray XL Crisper Tray with cooking spray and place the breaded olives on the Crisper Tray. Slide the Crisper Tray into the corresponding shelf position. Shake olives halfway through cooking according to the Shake Indicator.
7. When the cooking time has completed, transfer the olives to a plate. Cool before serving.

Spiced Sweet Potato Fries

SERVES 2

PREP TIME: 10 minutes
COOK TIME: 15 minutes

cooking spray
2 tbsps. olive oil
2 medium sweet potatoes (about 10 ounces / 284 g each), cut into wedges, ½ inch thick and 3 inches long
1½ tsps. kosher salt, plus more as needed
1½ tsps. smoked paprika
1 tsp. chili powder

½ tsp. ground turmeric
½ tsp. ground cumin
½ tsp. mustard powder
¼ tsp. cayenne pepper
Freshly ground black pepper, to taste
⅔ cup sour cream
1 garlic clove, grated

1. In a large bowl, combine the olive oil, paprika, salt, chili powder, cumin, turmeric, mustard powder, and cayenne.
2. Add the sweet potatoes, season with black pepper, and toss to coat well.
3. Insert the Drip Tray inside the appliance. Do not insert the Divider.
4. Use the left Control Knob to select Air Fry. Set the cooking temperature to 400°F and the cooking time to 15 minutes. Set the Shake Indicator and press the Start/Pause Button. Let the appliance preheat.
5. When the appliance has preheated, spray XL Crisper Tray with cooking spray and place the sweet potatoes on the Crisper Tray (save the bowl with the leftover oil and spices). Slide the Crisper Tray into the corresponding shelf position. Shake sweet potatoes halfway through cooking according to the Shake Indicator.
6. Meanwhile, in a small bowl, stir together the sour cream and garlic. Season with salt and black pepper and transfer to a serving dish.
7. When the cooking time has completed, return the sweet potato wedges to the reserved bowl and toss again while they are hot.
8. Serve the sweet potato wedges hot with the garlic sour cream.

Seasoned Pita Chips

SERVES 4

PREP TIME: 5 minutes
COOK TIME: 6 minutes

Cooking spray
2 whole grain 6-inch pitas
¼ tsp. dried basil
¼ tsp. marjoram
¼ tsp. ground thyme
¼ tsp. ground oregano
¼ tsp. garlic powder
¼ tsp. salt

1. Mix all the seasonings together.
2. Cut each pita half into 4 wedges. Break apart wedges at the fold.
3. Mist one side of pita wedges with oil. Sprinkle with half of seasoning mixture.
4. Turn the pita wedges over, mist the other side with oil, and sprinkle with remaining seasonings.
5. Insert the Drip Tray inside the appliance. Do not insert the Divider.
6. Use the left Control Knob to select Air Fry. Set the cooking temperature to 330°F and the cooking time to 6 minutes. Set the Shake Indicator and press the Start/Pause Button. Let the appliance preheat.
7. When the appliance has preheated, place the pita wedges on the XL Crisper Tray. Slide the Crisper Tray into the corresponding shelf position. Shake pita wedges halfway through cooking according to the Shake Indicator.
8. When the cooking time has completed, serve hot.

Spiced Mixed Nuts

MAKES 2 CUPS

PREP TIME: 5 minutes
COOK TIME: 6 minutes

cooking spray
2 tbsps. olive oil
½ cup raw pecan halves
½ cup raw cashews
½ cup raw whole almonds
½ cup raw walnut halves
1 tbsp. light brown sugar

1 tsp. chopped fresh thyme leaves
1 tsp. chopped fresh rosemary leaves
1 tsp. kosher salt
½ tsp. ground coriander
¼ tsp. onion powder
¼ tsp. freshly ground black pepper
⅛ tsp. garlic powder

1. In a large bowl, combine all the ingredients and toss until the nuts are well coated in the herbs, spices, and sugar.
2. Insert the Drip Tray inside the appliance. Do not insert the Divider.
3. Use the left Control Knob to select Air Fry. Set the cooking temperature to 350°F and the cooking time to 6 minutes. Set the Shake Indicator and press the Start/Pause Button. Let the appliance preheat.
4. When the appliance has preheated, spray XL Crisper Tray with cooking spray and scrape the nuts and seasonings on the Crisper Tray. Slide the Crisper Tray into the corresponding shelf position. Shake nuts halfway through cooking according to the Shake Indicator. Cook until the nuts are golden brown and fragrant.
5. When the cooking time has completed, transfer the cocktail nuts to a bowl and serve warm.

Cheesy Apple Roll-Ups

MAKES 8 ROLL-UPS

PREP TIME: 5 minutes
COOK TIME: 7 minutes

cooking spray
2 tbsps. butter, melted
½ small apple, chopped
8 slices whole wheat sandwich bread
4 ounces (113 g) Colby Jack cheese, grated

1. Remove the crusts from the bread and flatten the slices with a rolling pin. Don't be gentle. Press hard so that bread will be very thin.
2. Top the bread slices with cheese and chopped apple, dividing the ingredients evenly.
3. Roll up each slice tightly and secure each with one or two toothpicks.
4. Brush outside of rolls with melted butter.
5. Insert the Drip Tray inside the appliance. Do not insert the Divider.
6. Spray XL Crisper Tray with cooking spray. Place the rolls in a single layer on the Crisper Tray and slide the Crisper Tray into the corresponding shelf position.
7. Use the left Control Knob to select Bake. Set the cooking temperature to 390°F and the cooking time to 7 minutes. Press the Start/Pause Button to begin the cooking cycle.
8. When the cooking time has completed, transfer the rolls to a plate. Serve warm.

Rosemary-Garlic Shoestring Fries

SERVES 2

PREP TIME: 5 minutes
COOK TIME: 18 minutes

cooking spray
1 tbsp. vegetable oil
1 large russet potato (about 12 ounces / 340 g), scrubbed clean, and julienned
1 garlic clove, thinly sliced
Leaves from 1 sprig fresh rosemary
Kosher salt and freshly ground black pepper, to taste
Flaky sea salt, for serving

1. Place the julienned potatoes in a large colander and rinse under cold running water until the water runs clear. Spread the potatoes out on a double-thick layer of paper towels and pat dry.
2. In a large bowl, combine the potatoes, vegetable oil, and rosemary. Season with kosher salt and pepper to taste and toss to coat evenly.
3. Insert the Drip Tray inside the appliance. Do not insert the Divider.
4. Use the left Control Knob to select Air Fry. Set the cooking temperature to 400°F and the cooking time to 18 minutes. Set the Shake Indicator and press the Start/Pause Button. Let the appliance preheat.
5. When the appliance has preheated, spray XL Crisper Tray with cooking spray and place the potatoes on the Crisper Tray. Slide the Crisper Tray into the corresponding shelf position. Shake potatoes halfway through cooking according to the Shake Indicator.
6. With 5 minutes remaining, press the Start/Pause Button, shake for 10 seconds and add the garlic, and press the Start/Pause Button again to continue cooking.
7. When the cooking time has completed, transfer the fries to a plate and sprinkle with flaky sea salt while they're hot. Serve immediately.

Air Fried Pot Stickers

MAKES 30 POT STICKERS

PREP TIME: 10 minutes
COOK TIME: 12 minutes

cooking spray
30 wonton wrappers
1 egg, beaten
½ cup finely chopped cabbage
¼ cup finely chopped red bell pepper
2 green onions, finely chopped
2 tbsps. cocktail sauce
2 tsps. low-sodium soy sauce
1 tbsp. water, for brushing the wrappers

1. In a small bowl, combine the egg, cabbage, red bell pepper, green onions, cocktail sauce, and soy sauce, and mix well.
2. Put about 1 tsp. of the mixture in the center of each wonton wrapper. Fold the wrapper in half, covering the filling; dampen the edges with water, and seal. You can crimp the edges of the wrapper with your fingers so they look like the pot stickers you get in restaurants. Brush them with water.
3. Insert the Drip Tray inside the appliance. Do not insert the Divider.
4. Use the left Control Knob to select Air Fry. Set the cooking temperature to 360°F and the cooking time to 12 minutes. Set the Shake Indicator and press the Start/Pause Button. Let the appliance preheat.
5. When the appliance has preheated, spray XL Crisper Tray with cooking spray and place the pot stickers on the Crisper Tray. Slide the Crisper Tray into the corresponding shelf position. Shake pot stickers halfway through cooking according to the Shake Indicator. Cook until the pot stickers are hot and the bottoms are lightly browned.
6. When the cooking time has completed, serve hot.

Rosemary Cashews

PREP TIME: 5 minutes COOK TIME: 5 minutes	Cooking spray 2 cups roasted and unsalted whole cashews 2 sprigs of fresh rosemary (1 chopped and 1 whole)	1 tsp. olive oil 1 tsp. kosher salt ½ tsp. honey

1. In a medium bowl, whisk together the olive oil, chopped rosemary, kosher salt, and honey. Keep aside.
2. Insert the Drip Tray inside the appliance. Do not insert the Divider.
3. Spray XL Baking Pan with cooking spray and place the cashews and the whole rosemary sprig. Slide the Baking Pan into the corresponding shelf position.
4. Use the left Control Knob to select Roast. Set the cooking temperature to 300°F and the cooking time to 5 minutes. Press the Start/Pause Button to begin the cooking cycle, flipping halfway through cooking.
5. When the cooking time has completed, discard the rosemary and transfer the cashews to the olive oil mixture, tossing to coat well. Let cool for 15 minutes before serving.

Cajun Pickle Chips

PREP TIME: 5 minutes COOK TIME: 7 minutes	Cooking spray 2 large dill pickles, sliced into 8 rounds each ½ cup panko bread crumbs	¼ cup all-purpose flour 1 large egg, beaten 2 tsps. Cajun seasoning

1. Place the flour, bread crumbs, and egg into 3 separate shallow bowls, then stir the Cajun seasoning into the flour.
2. Dredge each pickle chip in the flour mixture, then the egg, and finally the bread crumbs. Shake off any excess, then place each coated pickle chip on a plate.
3. Insert the Drip Tray inside the appliance. Do not insert the Divider.
4. Use the left Control Knob to select Air Fry. Set the cooking temperature to 390°F and the cooking time to 7 minutes. Set the Shake Indicator and press the Start/Pause Button. Let the appliance preheat.
5. When the appliance has preheated, spray XL Crisper Tray with cooking spray and place the pickle chips in a single layer on the Crisper Tray. Slide the Crisper Tray into the corresponding shelf position. Shake pickle chips halfway through cooking according to the Shake Indicator.
6. When the cooking time has completed, transfer pickle chips to a plate and let cool slightly on a wire rack before serving.

Spinach and Crab Cups

PREP TIME: 10 minutes
COOK TIME: 7 minutes
	Cooking spray
	1 (6-ounce / 170-g) can crab meat,
	  drained to yield ⅓ cup meat
	30 mini frozen phyllo shells,
	  thawed
	¼ cup frozen spinach, thawed,
	  drained, and chopped
		½ cup grated Parmesan cheese
		3 tbsps. plain yogurt
		1 clove garlic, minced
		¼ tsp. lemon juice
		½ tsp. Worcestershire sauce

1. Remove any bits of shell that might remain in the crab meat.
2. Mix the crab meat, spinach, garlic, and cheese together in a bowl.
3. Stir in the yogurt, lemon juice, and Worcestershire sauce and combine well.
4. Spoon a tsp. of filling into each phyllo shell.
5. Insert the Drip Tray inside the appliance. Do not insert the Divider.
6. Spray XL Crisper Tray with cooking spray. Place the shells on the Crisper Tray and slide the Crisper Tray into the corresponding shelf position.
7. Use the left Control Knob to select Bake. Set the cooking temperature to 390°F and the cooking time to 7 minutes. Press the Start/Pause Button to begin the cooking cycle.
8. When the cooking time has completed, transfer the shells to a plate. Serve warm.

CHAPTER 11
DESSERT

Rice Pudding with Raisin

PREP TIME: 5 minutes
COOK TIME: 5 hours

2 tbsps. coconut oil
1⅔ cups brown Arborio rice
6 cups canned coconut milk
3 cups water
1 cup dark chocolate chips (optional)
1 cup raisins
½ cup coconut sugar
1 tbsp. vanilla extract

1. Mix the coconut milk and water in a 6-quart casserole dish. Place the rice and coconut sugar and combine well. Pour in the coconut oil and raisins.
2. Insert the Drip Tray inside the appliance. Do not insert the Divider.
3. Slide the Oven Rack into the corresponding shelf position. Place the casserole dish on the Oven Rack.
4. Use the left Control Knob to select Slow Cook. Set the cooking temperature to 225°F and the cooking time to 5 hours. Press the Start/Pause Button to begin the cooking cycle, until the rice is very soft.
5. When the cooking time has completed, gently stir in the vanilla. Sprinkle the pudding with chocolate chips, if using. Serve hot.

Cream Raspberry Cupcakes

PREP TIME: 10 minutes
COOK TIME: 20 minutes

cooking spray
2 eggs
½ cup fresh raspberries
4½-ounce self-rising flour
4¼-ounce caster sugar
4¾-ounce butter, softened
½-ounce cream cheese, softened
Pinch of salt
2 tsps. fresh lemon juice

1. Spray 10 silicon cups with cooking spray lightly.
2. Mix the flour, baking powder and salt in a small bowl.
3. Combine the cream cheese, sugar, eggs and butter in another bowl.
4. Mix the flour mixture with the cream cheese mixture and squeeze in the lemon juice.
5. Transfer the mixture into 10 silicon cups and top each cup with 2 raspberries.
6. Insert the Drip Tray inside the appliance. Do not insert the Divider.
7. Place the silicon cups on the XL Baking Pan. Slide the Baking Pan into the corresponding shelf position.
8. Use the left Control Knob to select Bake. Set the cooking temperature to 365°F and the cooking time to 20 minutes. Press the Start/Pause Button to begin the cooking cycle.
9. When the cooking time has completed, transfer the cups to a plate and enjoy.

Homemade Pecan Pie

PREP TIME: 10 minutes
COOK TIME: 35 minutes

cooking spray
⅓ cup butter, melted
1 frozen pie crust, thawed
2 large eggs
1 cup pecan halves
¾ cup brown sugar
¼ cup caster sugar
1¾ tbsps. flour
1 tsp. vanilla extract

1. Grease a 5-inch pie pan lightly with cooking spray.
2. Mix both sugars, eggs and butter in a medium bowl until smooth.
3. Stir in the flour, milk and vanilla extract and beat until well combined.
4. Gently fold in the pecan halves and arrange the crust in the bottom of pie pan. Put the pecan mixture in pie crust evenly.
5. Insert the Drip Tray inside the appliance. Do not insert the Divider.
6. Place the pie pan on the XL Baking Pan. Slide the Baking Pan into the corresponding shelf position.
7. Use the left Control Knob to select Bake. Set the cooking temperature to 300°F and the cooking time to 35 minutes. Press the Start/Pause Button to begin the cooking cycle.
8. When the cooking time has completed, let the pecan pie cool slightly and serve.

Chocolate Brownies

PREP TIME: 7 minutes
COOK TIME: 5 hours

5 tbsps. melted coconut oil
4 eggs
1½ cups whole-wheat pastry flour
1 cup mashed peeled ripe pears
1 cup mashed ripe bananas (about 2 medium)
¾ cup unsweetened cocoa powder
½ cup honey
½ cup coconut sugar
2 tsps. vanilla extract
1 tsp. baking powder

1. Tear off two long strips of heavy-duty foil and gently fold to make long thin strips. Put in a 6-quart casserole dish to make an X. Then line the casserole dish with parchment paper on top of the foil.
2. In a medium bowl, combine the pastry flour, baking powder and cocoa powder, and stir to combine well.
3. In another medium bowl, mix the melted coconut oil, mashed bananas, mashed pears, eggs, honey, coconut sugar and vanilla and combine well.
4. Pour the banana mixture into the flour mixture just until combined.
5. Scoop the batter into the casserole dish onto the parchment paper.
6. Insert the Drip Tray inside the appliance. Do not insert the Divider.
7. Slide the Oven Rack into the corresponding shelf position. Place the casserole dish on the Oven Rack.
8. Use the left Control Knob to select Slow Cook. Set the cooking temperature to 225°F and the cooking time to 4 hours. Press the Start/Pause Button to begin the cooking cycle, until a toothpick inserted near the center comes out with just a few moist crumbs attached to it.
9. When the cooking time has completed, gently remove the brownie with the foil sling. Let cool, then transfer the brownie from the parchment paper and cut into squares to serve.

Cinnamon Apple Cake

PREP TIME: 10 minutes
COOK TIME: 45 minutes

5 tbsps. plus 1 tsp. vegetable oil
2 cups apples, peeled, cored and chopped
1 cup all-purpose flour
1 egg
⅓ cup brown sugar

½ tsp. baking soda
1 tsp. ground nutmeg
1 tsp. ground cinnamon
¾ tsp. vanilla extract
Salt, to taste

1. Grease a 7 x 5-inch baking dish lightly.
2. Mix the flour, sugar, spices, baking soda and salt in a bowl until well combined.
3. Whisk the egg with oil and vanilla extract in another bowl.
4. Stir in the flour mixture gently and fold in the apples.
5. Pour this mixture into the greased baking dish and cover with the foil paper.
6. Insert the Drip Tray inside the appliance. Do not insert the Divider.
7. Place the baking dish on the XL Baking Pan. Slide the Baking Pan into the corresponding shelf position.
8. Use the left Control Knob to select Bake. Set the cooking temperature to 355°F and the cooking time to 45 minutes. Press the Start/Pause Button to begin the cooking cycle.
9. With 5 minutes remaining, press the Start/Pause Button, remove the foil and press the Start/Pause Button again to continue cooking.
10. When the cooking time has completed, let cool for 20 minutes and cut into slices to serve.

Chocolate Molten Cake

PREP TIME: 5 minutes
COOK TIME: 12 minutes

2 eggs
3.5 ounces (99 g) butter, melted
3.5 ounces (99 g) chocolate, melted
3½ tbsps. sugar
1½ tbsps. flour

1. Grease four 3-inch ramekins with a little butter.
2. Rigorously combine the eggs, butter and sugar before stirring in the melted chocolate.
3. Gently fold in the flour.
4. Spoon an equal amount of the mixture into each ramekin.
5. Insert the Drip Tray inside the appliance. Do not insert the Divider.
6. Place the ramekins on the XL Baking Pan. Slide the Baking Pan into the corresponding shelf position.
7. Use the left Control Knob to select Bake. Set the cooking temperature to 375°F and the cooking time to 12 minutes. Press the Start/Pause Button to begin the cooking cycle.
8. When the cooking time has completed, put the ramekins upside-down on plates and let the cakes fall out. Serve hot.

Pecan Eggnog Bread

SERVES 6

PREP TIME: 10 minutes
COOK TIME: 18 minutes

Cooking spray
1 cup flour, plus more for dusting
¼ cup sugar
1 tsp. baking powder
¼ tsp. salt
¼ tsp. nutmeg
½ cup eggnog
1 egg yolk
¼ cup pecans
¼ cup chopped candied fruit (cherries, pineapple, or mixed fruits)
1 tbsp. plus 1 tsp. butter, melted

1. In a medium bowl, stir together the flour, sugar, baking powder, salt, and nutmeg.
2. Add the eggnog, egg yolk, and butter. Mix well but do not beat.
3. Stir in the nuts and candied fruit.
4. Spray a 7 x 5-inch baking dish with cooking spray and dust with flour. Spread the batter into the prepared dish.
5. Insert the Drip Tray inside the appliance. Do not insert the Divider.
6. Place the dish on the XL Baking Pan. Slide the Baking Pan into the corresponding shelf position.
7. Use the left Control Knob to select Bake. Set the cooking temperature to 360°F and the cooking time to 18 minutes. Press the Start/Pause Button to begin the cooking cycle, until top is dark golden brown and bread starts to pull away from sides of dish.
8. When the cooking time has completed, serve immediately.

Flavor-Packed Clafoutis

SERVES 4

PREP TIME: 10 minutes
COOK TIME: 25 minutes

1½ cups fresh cherries, pitted
½ cup sour cream
¼ cup powdered sugar
¼ cup flour
1 egg
3 tbsps. vodka
2 tbsps. sugar
1 tbsp. butter
Pinch of salt

1. Grease a 7 x 5-inch baking dish lightly.
2. Mix the cherries and vodka in a medium bowl.
3. Sift together flour, sugar and salt in another bowl.
4. Stir in the sour cream and egg until a smooth dough is formed.
5. Transfer the dough evenly into the greased baking dish and top with the cherry mixture and butter.
6. Insert the Drip Tray inside the appliance. Do not insert the Divider.
7. Place the baking dish on the XL Baking Pan. Slide the Baking Pan into the corresponding shelf position.
8. Use the left Control Knob to select Bake. Set the cooking temperature to 355°F and the cooking time to 25 minutes. Press the Start/Pause Button to begin the cooking cycle.
9. When the cooking time has completed, dust with powdered sugar and serve warm.

Apple Dumplings

PREP TIME: 10 minutes COOK TIME: 25 minutes	cooking spray **2 small apples, peeled and cored** **2 sheets puff pastry** **2 tbsps. butter, melted** **2 tbsps. raisins** **1 tbsp. brown sugar**

1. Mix the sugar and raisins in a small bowl and fill each apple core with it.
2. Place the apple in the center of each pastry sheet and fold to completely cover the apple. Seal the edges.
3. Insert the Drip Tray inside the appliance. Do not insert the Divider.
4. Spray XL Crisper Tray with cooking spray. Place the dumplings on the Crisper Tray and slide the Crisper Tray into the corresponding shelf position.
5. Use the left Control Knob to select Bake. Set the cooking temperature to 355°F and the cooking time to 25 minutes. Press the Start/Pause Button to begin the cooking cycle.
6. When the cooking time has completed, transfer the dumplings to a platter and serve warm.

Classic Shortbread Fingers

PREP TIME: 10 minutes COOK TIME: 14 minutes	cooking spray **¾ cup butter** **1⅔ cups plain flour** **⅓ cup caster sugar**

1. Mix the sugar, flour and butter in a small bowl to form a dough.
2. Cut the dough into 10 equal sized fingers and prick the fingers lightly with a fork.
3. Insert the Drip Tray inside the appliance. Do not insert the Divider.
4. Spray XL Crisper Tray with cooking spray. Place the fingers on the Crisper Tray and slide the Crisper Tray into the corresponding shelf position.
5. Use the left Control Knob to select Bake. Set the cooking temperature to 355°F and the cooking time to 14 minutes. Press the Start/Pause Button to begin the cooking cycle.
6. When the cooking time has completed, serve warm.

Peach Parcel

PREP TIME: 10 minutes COOK TIME: 15 minutes	cooking spray **1 peach, peeled, cored and halved** **2 puff pastry sheets** **1 cup prepared vanilla custard**	**1 egg, beaten lightly** **1 tbsp. whipped cream** **1 tbsp. sugar** **Pinch of ground cinnamon**

1. Place a spoonful of vanilla custard and a peach half in the center of each pastry sheet.
2. Mix the sugar and cinnamon in a small bowl and sprinkle on the peach halves.
3. Pinch the corners of sheets together to shape into a parcel.
4. Insert the Drip Tray inside the appliance. Do not insert the Divider.
5. Spray XL Crisper Tray with cooking spray. Place the parcels on the Crisper Tray and slide the Crisper Tray into the corresponding shelf position.
6. Use the left Control Knob to select Bake. Set the cooking temperature to 340°F and the cooking time to 15 minutes. Press the Start/Pause Button to begin the cooking cycle.
7. When the cooking time has completed, top with whipped cream and serve with remaining custard.

APPENDIX 1:
EMERIL LAGASSE DUAL ZONE AIR FRYER

The Time and Temperature on the chart below refer the basic default settings. As you become familiar with the Unit, you will be able to make minor adjustments to suit your taste.

Settings	Default Temp (Temp Rang)	Default Time (Time Range)	Default Fan Speed	Preheating Included in Cooking Time
Air Fry	400°F (180°F-450°F)	20 mins (1-60 mins)	High	No
Roast	350°F (180°F-450°F)	35 mins (1 min-4 hrs)	Low	Yes
Broil	450°F (400°F-450°F)	10 mins (1-20 mins)	High	Yes
Bake	350°F (180°F-450°F)	25 mins (1 min-4 hrs)	Low	Yes
Pizza	400°F (180°F-450°F)	18 mins (1-60 mins)	Off	Yes
Grill	450°F (250°F-450°F)	15 mins (1-45 mins)	Off	Yes
Toast	(Light-Dark)	4 slices (1-6 slices)	Off	No
Reheat	280°F (180°F-450°F)	20 mins (1 min-2 hrs)	Low	No
Keep Warm	160°F (160°F-250°F)	1 hr (1 min-4 hrs)	Off	No
Dehydrate	120°F (85°F-175°F)	6 hrs (30 mins-72 hrs)	Low	No
Rotisserie	375°F (180°F-450°F)	40 mins (1 min-4 hrs)	High	Yes
Slow Cook	225°F (225°F-275°F)	4 hrs (30 mins-10 hrs)	Low	No

APPENDIX 2: 30-DAY MEAL PLAN

Meal Plan	Breakfast	Lunch	Dinner	Snack/Dessert
Day-1	Spanish Style Frittata	Cornish Game Hen	Sweet and Sour Chicken Thighs	Air Fried Green Olives
Day-2	Cheesy Mushroom Risotto	Lemon-Rosemary Roasted Chicken	Grilled Beef Burgers	Spiced Sweet Potato Fries
Day-3	Healthy Spinach Omelet	BBQ Chicken Wings	Chinese Style Cod	Seasoned Pita Chips
Day-4	Nut and Seed Muffins	Chicken with Veggies	Roasted Cod with Broccoli	Spinach and Crab Cups
Day-5	Pepperoni Pita Pizza	Herbed Beef Roast	Beef and Veggie Kebabs	Spiced Mixed Nuts
Day-6	Homemade Banana Bread	Chinese Chicken Drumsticks	Vegetable and White Fish Tacos	Pecan Eggnog Bread
Day-7	Tasty Toasts	Bacon Wrapped Filet Mignon	Baked Cheese Sandwich	Rice Pudding with Raisin
Day-8	Fast Coffee Donuts	Beef Bratwursts	Fajita Meatball Lettuce Wraps	Cream Raspberry Cupcakes
Day-9	Gold Avocado	Cajun-Style Salmon Burgers	Banana Egg Oatmeal Sandwich	Apple Dumplings
Day-10	Breadcrumbs Stuffed Mushrooms	Buttered Rib Eye Steak	Herbed Beef Roast	Classic Shortbread Fingers

Meal Plan	Breakfast	Lunch	Dinner	Snack/Dessert
Day-11	Buttermilk Biscuits	Crispy Chicken Tenders	Tasty London Broil	Cheesy Apple Roll-Ups
Day-12	Red Bell Peppers Cups	Chili Shrimps	Buttered Scallops	Pecan Eggnog Bread
Day-13	Garden Veggie Medley	Steak with Bell Peppers	Turkey, Hummus, and Cheese Wraps	Homemade Pecan Pie
Day-14	Buttered Broccoli	Marinated Salmon Fillets	Appetizing Chicken Pieces	Grilled Beef Burgers
Day-15	Smashed Potatoes with Thyme	Grilled Tuna Cakes	Mixed Greens Sandwich	Seasoned Pita Chips
Day-16	Honey Beets and Onions	Chinese Style Cod	Nugget and Corn Taco Wraps	Chocolate Brownies
Day-17	Spanish Style Frittata	Roasted Cod with Broccoli	Cheesy Chicken Sandwich	Flavor-Packed Clafoutis
Day-18	Gold Avocado	Mahi Mahi with Green Beans	Cheesy Shrimp Sandwich	Beef Bratwursts
Day-19	Healthy Spinach Omelet	BBQ Chicken Wings	Buttered Rib Eye Steak	Cinnamon Apple Cake
Day-20	Ham and Corn Muffins	Lemon-Rosemary Roasted Chicken	Tuna and Lettuce Wraps	Spinach and Crab Cups

Meal Plan	Breakfast	Lunch	Dinner	Snack/Dessert
Day-21	Nut and Seed Muffins	Bacon Wrapped Filet Mignon	Fantastic Leg of Lamb	Spicy Beef Jerky
Day-22	Pepperoni Pita Pizza	Appetizing Chicken Pieces	Sweet and Sour Chicken Thighs	Cheesy Apple Roll-Ups
Day-23	Homemade Banana Bread	Chili Shrimps	Steak with Bell Peppers	Spiced Mixed Nuts
Day-24	Buttermilk Biscuits	Buttered Scallops	Lamb with Potatoes	Peach Parcel
Day-25	Cheesy Mushroom Risotto	Beef and Veggie Kebabs	Herbed Lamb Burger	Cream Raspberry Cupcakes
Day-26	Ham and Corn Muffins	Tasty London Broil	Za'atar Lamb Loin Chops	Homemade Pecan Pie
Day-27	Breadcrumbs Stuffed Mushrooms	Marinated Salmon Fillets	Marinated Pork	Chocolate Brownies
Day-28	Honey Beets and Onions	Chinese Chicken Drumsticks	Nut Crusted Rack of Lamb	Rice Pudding with Raisin
Day-29	Fast Coffee Donuts	Crispy Chicken Tenders	Chicken with Veggies	Classic Shortbread Fingers
Day-30	Tasty Toasts	Cajun-Style Salmon Burgers	Garlicky Lamb Chops	Apple Dumplings

APPENDIX 3:
BASIC KITCHEN CONVERSIONS & EQUIVALENTS

DRY MEASUREMENTS CONVERSION CHART

3 teaspoons = 1 tablespoon = 1/16 cup
6 teaspoons = 2 tablespoons = 1/8 cup
12 teaspoons = 4 tablespoons = ¼ cup
24 teaspoons = 8 tablespoons = ½ cup
36 teaspoons = 12 tablespoons = ¾ cup
48 teaspoons = 16 tablespoons = 1 cup

METRIC TO US COOKING CONVERSIONS

OVEN TEMPERATURES

120 ºC = 250 ºF
160 ºC = 320 ºF
180 ºC = 350 ºF
205 ºC = 400 ºF
220 ºC = 425 ºF

LIQUID MEASUREMENTS CONVERSION CHART

8 fluid ounces = 1 cup = ½ pint = ¼ quart
16 fluid ounces = 2 cups = 1 pint = ½ quart
32 fluid ounces = 4 cups = 2 pints = 1 quart = ¼ gallon
128 fluid ounces = 16 cups = 8 pints = 4 quarts = 1 gallon

BAKING IN GRAMS

1 cup flour = 140 grams
1 cup sugar = 150 grams
1 cup powdered sugar = 160 grams
1 cup heavy cream = 235 grams

VOLUME

1 milliliter = 1/5 teaspoon
5 ml = 1 teaspoon
15 ml = 1 tablespoon
240 ml = 1 cup or 8 fluid ounces
1 liter = 34 fluid ounces

WEIGHT

1 gram = .035 ounces
100 grams = 3.5 ounces
500 grams = 1.1 pounds
1 kilogram = 35 ounces

US TO METRIC COOKING CONVERSIONS

1/5 tsp = 1 ml
1 tsp = 5 ml
1 tbsp = 15 ml
1 fluid ounces = 30 ml
1 cup = 237 ml
1 pint (2 cups) = 473 ml
1 quart (4 cups) = .95 liter
1 gallon (16 cups) = 3.8 liters
1 oz = 28 grams
1 pound = 454 grams

BUTTER

1 cup butter = 2 sticks = 8 ounces = 230 grams = 16 tablespoons

WHAT DOES 1 CUP EQUAL

1 cup = 8 fluid ounces
1 cup = 16 tablespoons
1 cup = 48 teaspoons
1 cup = ½ pint
1 cup = ¼ quart
1 cup = 1/16 gallon
1 cup = 240 ml

BAKING PAN CONVERSIONS

9-inch round cake pan = 12 cups
10-inch tube pan =16 cups
10-inch bundt pan = 12 cups
9-inch springform pan = 10 cups
9 x 5 inch loaf pan = 8 cups
9-inch square pan = 8 cups

BAKING PAN CONVERSIONS

1 cup all-purpose flour = 4.5 oz
1 cup rolled oats = 3 oz
1 large egg = 1.7 oz
1 cup butter = 8 oz
1 cup milk = 8 oz
1 cup heavy cream = 8.4 oz
1 cup granulated sugar = 7.1 oz
1 cup packed brown sugar = 7.75 oz
1 cup vegetable oil = 7.7 oz
1 cup unsifted powdered sugar = 4.4 oz

APPENDIX 4:
RECIPES INDEX

Made in United States
Orlando, FL
20 November 2024

54143532R00043